Ferrari
312P & 312PB

Other great books from Veloce –

Rally Giants Series
Audi Quattro (Robson)
Austin Healey 100-6 & 3000 (Robson)
Fiat 131 Abarth (Robson)
Ford Escort MkI (Robson)
Ford Escort RS Cosworth & World Rally Car (Robson)
Ford Escort RS1800 (Robson)
Lancia Delta 4WD/Integrale (Robson)
Lancia Stratos (Robson)
Mini Cooper/Mini Cooper S (Robson)
Peugeot 205 T16 (Robson)
Saab 96 & V4 (Robson)
Subaru Impreza (Robson)
Toyota Celica GT4 (Robson)

WSC Giants
Audi R8 (Wagstaff)
Ferrari 312P & 312PB (Collins & McDonough)
Gulf-Mirage 1967 to 1982 (McDonough)
Matra Sports Cars – MS620, 630, 650, 660 & 670 – 1966 to 1974 (McDonough)

General
1½-litre GP Racing 1961-1965 (Whitelock)
AC Two-litre Saloons & Buckland Sportscars (Archibald)
Alfa Romeo 155/156/147 Competition Touring Cars (Collins)
Alfa Romeo Giulia Coupé GT & GTA (Tipler)
Alfa Romeo Montreal – The dream car that came true (Taylor)
Alfa Romeo Montreal – The Essential Companion (Taylor)
Alfa Tipo 33 (McDonough & Collins)
Alpine & Renault – The Development of the Revolutionary Turbo F1 Car 1968 to 1979 (Smith)
Alpine & Renault – The Sports Prototypes 1963 to 1969 (Smith)
Alpine & Renault – The Sports Prototypes 1973 to 1978 (Smith)
Anatomy of the Works Minis (Moylan)
Armstrong-Siddeley (Smith)
Art Deco and British Car Design (Down)
Autodrome (Collins & Ireland)
Autodrome 2 (Collins & Ireland)
Automotive A-Z, Lane's Dictionary of Automotive Terms (Lane)
Automotive Mascots (Kay & Springate)
Bahamas Speed Weeks, The (O'Neil)
Bentley Continental, Corniche and Azure (Bennett)
Bentley MkVI, Rolls-Royce Silver Wraith, Dawn & Cloud/Bentley R & S-Series (Nutland)
Bluebird CN7 (Stevens)
BMC Competitions Department Secrets (Turner, Chambers & Browning)
BMW 5-Series (Cranswick)
BMW Z-Cars (Taylor)
BMW – The Power of M (Vivian)
Bonjour – Is this Italy? (Turner)
British 250cc Racing Motorcycles (Pereira)
British at Indianapolis, The (Wagstaff)
British Cars, The Complete Catalogue of, 1895-1975 (Culshaw & Horrobin)
BRM – A Mechanic's Tale (Salmon)
BRM V16 (Ludvigsen)
Bugatti Type 40 (Price)
Bugatti 46/50 Updated Edition (Price & Arbey)
Bugatti T44 & T49 (Price & Arbey)
Bugatti 57 2nd Edition (Price)
Carrera Panamericana, La (Tipler)
Chrysler 300 – America's Most Powerful Car 2nd Edition (Ackerson)
Chrysler PT Cruiser (Ackerson)
Citroën DS (Bobbitt)

Cobra – The Real Thing! (Legate)
Concept Cars, How to illustrate and design (Dewey)
Cortina – Ford's Bestseller (Robson)
Coventry Climax Racing Engines (Hammill)
Daily Mirror 1970 World Cup Rally 40, The (Robson)
Daimler SP250 New Edition (Long)
Datsun Fairlady Roadster to 280ZX – The Z-Car Story (Long)
Dino – The V6 Ferrari (Long)
Dodge Challenger & Plymouth Barracuda (Grist)
Dodge Charger – Enduring Thunder (Ackerson)
Dodge Dynamite! (Grist)
Draw & Paint Cars – How to (Gardiner)
Drive on the Wild Side, A – 20 Extreme Driving Adventures From Around the World (Weaver)
Dune Buggy, Building A – The Essential Manual (Shakespeare)
Dune Buggy Files (Hale)
Dune Buggy Handbook (Hale)
East German Motor Vehicles in Pictures (Suhr/Weinreich)
Fast Ladies – Female Racing Drivers 1888 to 1970 (Bouzanquet)
Fate of the Sleeping Beauties, The (op de Weegh/Hottendorff/op de Weegh)
Ferrari 288 GTO, The Book of the (Sackey)
Fiat & Abarth 124 Spider & Coupé (Long)
Fiat & Abarth 500 & 600 – 2nd Edition (Bobbitt)
Fiats, Great Small (Ward)
Fine Art of the Motorcycle Engine, The (Peirce)
Ford Cleveland 335-Series V8 engine 1970 to 1982 – The Essential Source Book (Hammill)
Ford F100/F150 Pick-up 1948-1996 (Ackerson)
Ford F150 Pick-up 1997-2005 (Ackerson)
Ford GT – Then, and Now (Streather)
Ford GT40 (Legate)
Ford Model Y (Roberts)
Ford Thunderbird From 1954, The Book of the (Long)
Formula 5000 Motor Racing, Back then ... and back now (Lawson)
Forza Minardi! (Vigar)
France: the essential guide for car enthusiasts – 200 things for the car enthusiast to see and do (Parish)
From Crystal Palace to Red Square – - A Hapless Biker's Road to Russia (Turner)
Funky Mopeds (Skelton)
Grand Prix Ferrari – The Years of Enzo Ferrari's Power, 1948-1980 (Pritchard)
Grand Prix Ford – DFV-powered Formula 1 Cars (Pritchard)
GT – The World's Best GT Cars 1953-73 (Dawson)
Hillclimbing & Sprinting – The Essential Manual (Short & Wilkinson)
Honda NSX (Long)
Intermeccanica – The Story of the Prancing Bull (McCredie & Reisner)
Jaguar, The Rise of (Price)
Jaguar XJ 220 – The Inside Story (Moreton)
Jaguar XJ-S, The Book of the (Long)
Jeep CJ (Ackerson)
Jeep Wrangler (Ackerson)
Karmann-Ghia Coupé & Convertible (Bobbitt)
Kris Meeke – Intercontinental Rally Challenge Champion (McBride)
Lamborghini Miura Bible, The (Sackey)
Lamborghini Urraco, The Book of the (Landsem)
Lancia 037 (Collins)
Lancia Delta HF Integrale (Blaettel & Wagner)
Land Rover Series III Reborn (Porter)
Land Rover, The Half-ton Military (Cook)
Lea-Francis Story, The (Price)
Le Mans Panoramic (Ireland)
Lexus Story, The (Long)

Little book of microcars, the (Quellin)
Little book of smart, the – New Edition (Jackson)
Little book of trikes, the (Quellin)
Lola – The Illustrated History (1957-1977) (Starkey)
Lola – All the Sports Racing & Single-seater Racing Cars 1978-1997 (Starkey)
Lola T70 – The Racing History & Individual Chassis Record – 4th Edition (Starkey)
Lotus 49 (Oliver)
Marketingmobiles, The Wonderful Wacky World of (Hale)
Maserati 250F In Focus (Pritchard)
Mazda MX-5/Miata 1.6 Enthusiast's Workshop Manual (Grainger & Shoemark)
Mazda MX-5/Miata 1.8 Enthusiast's Workshop Manual (Grainger & Shoemark)
Mazda MX-5 Miata: The Book of the World's Favourite Sportscar (Long)
Mazda MX-5 Miata Roadster (Long)
Maximum Mini (Booij)
Meet the English (Bowie)
Mercedes-Benz SL – W113-series 1963-1971 (Long)
Mercedes-Benz SL & SLC – 107-series 1971-1989 (Long)
Mercedes-Benz SLK – R170 series 1996-2004 (Long)
MGA (Price Williams)
Micro Trucks (Mort)
Microcars at Large! (Quellin)
Mini Cooper – The Real Thing! (Tipler)
Mini Minor to Asia Minor (West)
Mitsubishi Lancer Evo, The Road Car & WRC Story (Long)
Monthléry, The Story of the Paris Autodrome (Boddy)
Morgan Maverick (Lawrence)
Morris Minor, 60 Years on the Road (Newell)
Moto Guzzi Sport & Le Mans Bible, The (Falloon)
Motor Movies – The Posters! (Veysey)
Motor Racing – Reflections of a Lost Era (Carter)
Motor Racing – The Pursuit of Victory 1930-1962 (Carter)
Motor Racing – The Pursuit of Victory 1963-1972 (Wyatt/Sears)
Motor Racing Heroes – The Stories of 100 Greats (Newman)
Motorcycle GP Racing in the 1960s (Pereira)
Motorsport In colour, 1950s (Wainwright)
Nissan 300ZX & 350Z – The Z-Car Story (Long)
Nissan GT-R Supercar: Born to race (Gorodji)
Northeast American Sports Car Races 1950-1959 (O'Neil)
Nothing Runs – Misadventures in the Classic, Collectable & Exotic Car Biz (Slutsky)
Off-Road Giants! (Volume 1) – Heroes of 1960s Motorcycle Sport (Westlake)
Off-Road Giants! (Volume 2) – Heroes of 1960s Motorcycle Sport (Westlake)
Pass the Theory and Practical Driving Tests (Gibson & Hoole)
Peking to Paris 2007 (Young)
Pontiac Firebird (Cranswick)
Porsche Boxster (Long)
Porsche 356 (2nd Edition) (Long)
Porsche 908 (Födisch, Neßhöver, Roßbach, Schwarz & Roßbach)
Porsche 911 Carrera – The Last of the Evolution (Corlett)
Porsche 911, RS & RSR, 4th Edition (Starkey)
Porsche 911, The Book of the (Long)
Porsche 911SC 'Super Carrera' – The Essential Companion (Streather)
Porsche 914 & 914-6: The Definitive History of the Road & Competition Cars (Long)
Porsche 924 (Long)
The Porsche 924 Carreras - evolution to excellence (Smith)
Porsche 928 (Long)
Porsche 944 (Long)

Porsche 964, 993 & 996 Data Plate Code Breaker (Streather)
Porsche 993 'King Of Porsche' – The Essential Companion (Streather)
Porsche 996 'Supreme Porsche' – The Essential Companion (Streather)
Porsche Racing Cars – 1953 to 1975 (Long)
Porsche Racing Cars – 1976 to 2005 (Long)
Porsche – The Rally Story (Meredith)
Porsche: Three Generations of Genius (Meredith)
Preston Tucker & Others (Linde)
RAC Rally Action! (Gardiner)
Racing Colours – Motor Racing Compositions 1908-2009 (Newman)
Rallye Sport Fords: The Inside Story (Moreton)
Roads with a View – England's greatest views and how to find them by road (Corfield)
Roads With a View – Wales' greatest views and how to find them by road (Corfield)
Rolls-Royce Silver Shadow/Bentley T Series Corniche & Camargue – Revised & Enlarged Edition (Bobbitt)
Rolls-Royce Silver Spirit, Silver Spur & Bentley Mulsanne 2nd Edition (Bobbitt)
Runways & Racers (O'Neil)
Russian Motor Vehicles – Soviet Limousines 1930-2003 (Kelly)
Russian Motor Vehicles – The Czarist Period 1784 to 1917 (Kelly)
RX-7 – Mazda's Rotary Engine Sportscar (Updated & Revised New Edition) (Long)
Scooters & Microcars, The A-Z of Popular (Dan)
Scooter Lifestyle (Grainger)
Singer Story: Cars, Commercial Vehicles, Bicycles & Motorcycle (Atkinson)
Sleeping Beauties USA – abandoned classic cars & trucks (Marek)
SM – Citroën's Maserati-engined Supercar (Long & Claverol)
Speedway – Auto racing's ghost tracks (Collins & Ireland)
Sprite Caravans, The Story of (Jenkinson)
Standard Motor Company, The Book of the
Subaru Impreza: The Road Car And WRC Story (Long)
Supercar, How to Build your own (Thompson)
Tales from the Toolbox (Oliver)
Taxi! The Story of the 'London' Taxicab (Bobbitt)
Toleman Story, The (Hilton)
Toyota Celica & Supra, The Book of Toyota's Sports Coupés (Long)
Toyota MR2 Coupés & Spyders (Long)
Triumph TR6 (Kimberley)
TT Talking – The TT's most exciting era – As seen by Manx Radio TT's lead commentator 2004-2012 (Lambert)
TWR Story, The – Group A (Hughes & Scott)
Unraced (Collins)
Velocette Motorcycles – MSS to Thruxton – New Third Edition (Burris)
Volkswagen Bus Book, The (Bobbitt)
Volkswagen Bus or Van to Camper, How to Convert (Porter)
Volkswagens of the World (Glen)
VW Beetle Cabriolet – The full story of the convertible Beetle (Bobbitt)
VW Beetle – The Car of the 20th Century (Copping)
VW Bus – 40 Years of Splitties, Bays & Wedges (Copping)
VW Bus Book, The (Bobbitt)
VW Golf: Five Generations of Fun (Copping & Cservenka)
VW – The Air-cooled Era (Copping)
VW T5 Camper Conversion Manual (Porter)
VW Campers (Copping)
Which Oil? – Choosing the right oils & greases for your antique, vintage, veteran, classic or collector car (Michell)
Works Minis, The Last (Purves & Brenchley)
Works Rally Mechanic (Moylan)

www.veloce.co.uk

For post publication news, updates and amendments relating to this book please visit www.veloce.co.uk/books/V4259

First published in August 2009, reprinted May 2014 by Veloce Publishing Limited, Veloce House, Parkway Farm Business Park, Middle Farm Way, Poundbury, Dorchester DT1 3AR, England. Fax 01305 268864/e-mail info@veloce.co.uk/web www.velocebooks.com.
ISBN: 978-1-845842-59-8 UPC: 6-36847-04259-2
© Ed McDonough and Peter Collins and Veloce Publishing 2009 & 2014. All rights reserved. With the exception of quoting brief passages for the purpose of review, no part of this publication may be recorded, reproduced or transmitted by any means, including photocopying, without the written permission of Veloce Publishing Ltd. Throughout this book logos, model names and designations, etc, have been used for the purposes of identification, illustration and decoration. Such names are the property of the trademark holder as this is not an official publication.
Readers with ideas for automotive books, or books on other transport or related hobby subjects, are invited to write to the editorial director of Veloce Publishing at the above address.
British Library Cataloguing in Publication Data – A catalogue record for this book is available from the British Library. Typesetting, design and page make-up all by Veloce Publishing Ltd on Apple Mac. Printed in India by Imprint Digital.

Ferrari
312P & 312PB

WSC GIANTS

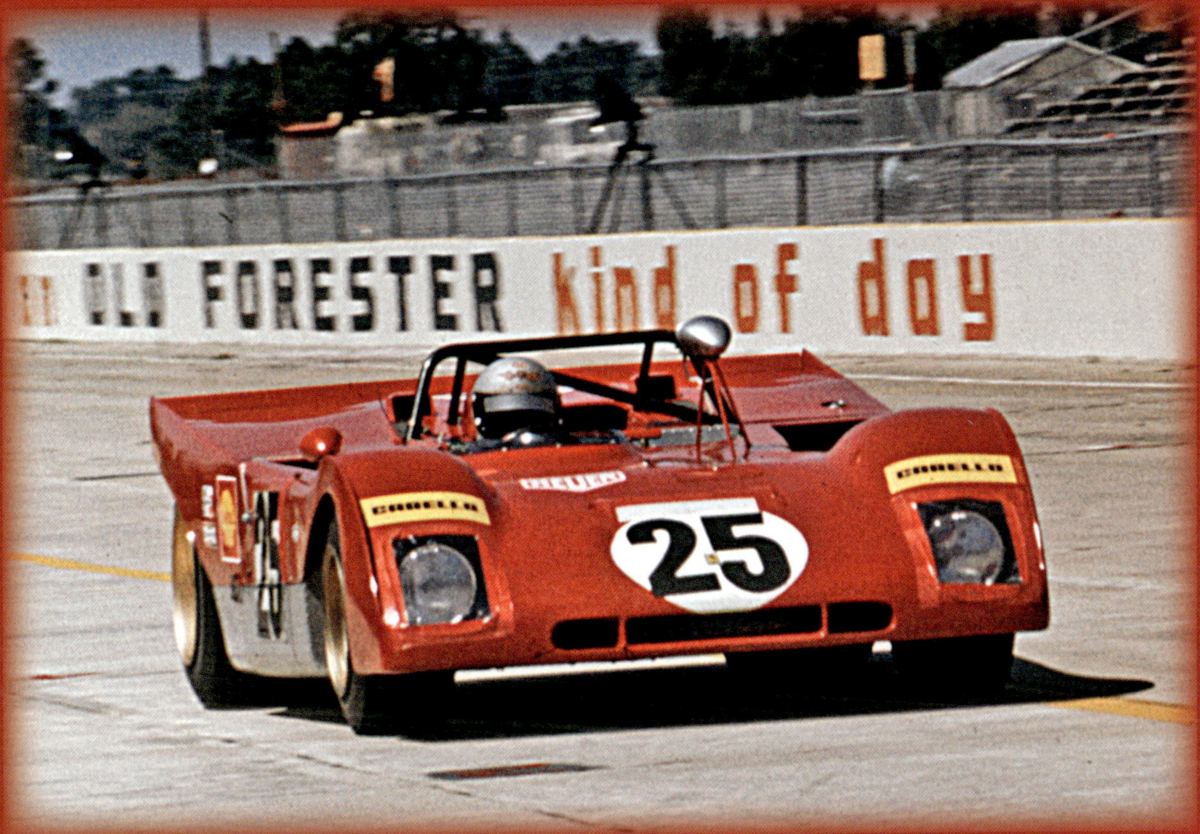

Ed McDonough & Peter Collins

Contents

Introduction 5

Acknowledgements 6

The 1969/1970 Ferrari 312P V-12 – The beginning 7

1970 – No works Ferraris 24

1971 – 312P Ferrari flat-12 – The life of a 312P 37

1972 – Ferrari 312PB flat-12 – Packing a punch 69

1973 – Ferrari 312PB flat-12 – Ides of March 97

Appendix 1 – List of races 117

Appendix 2 – The cars today 121

Bibliography 122

Index 127

Introduction

Sports car racing has embraced a wide variety of forms in its long history. Since the first formal Championship was inaugurated in 1953, the World Sports Car Championship, there have been some thirty-three different series (Wimpffen, 1999, p.27). While much of the period since has been characterised by vehicles built to resemble, at least to a degree, cars built for the roads, competing cars have always had an in-built tendency to become more like racing cars than passenger vehicles. The rules formulated by international bodies, particularly the FIA, have attempted, with varying levels of success, to force constraints that control the technical development of these cars. Sports car racing history is really the tale of how difficult that process has always been.

The main ingredients of the rules, especially in the early days, were almost always engine size, and then increasingly specific restrictions which attempted to define what a 'sports car' or a 'sports racing car' was. At the very first Championship event, the 1953 Sebring 12 Hours, there were classes for cars with engines from 5 to 8 litres, 3 to 5 litres, 2 to 3 litres, 1.5 to 2 litres, 1.1 to 1.5 litres, 750cc to 1.1 litres and up to 750cc. The FIA agreed as many as 15 different displacement categories during these early years. Individual organisers, especially at events such as Le Mans, would add their own specific regulations. Sometimes these were complementary to FIA rules and sometimes they either conflicted or confused. The ACO at Le Mans devised the most complex and difficult rules for windscreens in the history of the sport. These conflicts sometimes saw the unity of Championships fall apart. In 1956, Le Mans was separate from the World Sports Car Championship and ran to its own rules for the Le Mans Endurance Classic. It is also important to note that the series were almost always championships for manufacturers rather than for drivers.

The initial series was followed by the FIA Grand Touring Cup (1960-61), World Manufacturers' Championship for Grand Touring Cars (1962-65), Challenge Mondiale de Vitesse et Endurance (1962-74 ... some of these series overlapped with others), FIA Prototype Grand Touring Trophy (1963-65), International Trophy for Prototypes (1966-67), International Makes Championship for Sports Cars (1966-67), Endurance Classics Triple Crown (1966-71, 1973, 1975-99), International Championship of Makes (1968-71), and the World Championship of Makes (1972-75). The latter two Championships are the ones with which this book is concerned, though, indeed, they evolved from the previous series, which marked a move away from GT cars to Prototypes, a swing that was eventually reversed.

Visit Veloce on the web – www.veloce.co.uk
Details of all books in print • Special offers • New book news • Gift vouchers • Web forum • And much more ...

Acknowledgements

I would first like to thank my hard-working co-author, Peter Collins, for his significant contribution both to the text and to the photographic record in this book. His long-term interest in and knowledge of sports cars, especially Ferraris, is the solid foundation of this volume. We have worked together on many occasions, and readers will see that we were both at many of the same races in period!

We also must acknowledge the fine photo contributions of several other people. Notably these include Pete Austin ... I think we must have been standing next to him in 1969 as well. Thanks also go to: Casey Annis, for photos and the use of his interview with Tony Adamowicz, Richard Bunyan, Sergio Febbraro, Louis Galanos, Bob Graham, Brian Joscelyne, Dave Kutz, Fred Lewis, Paul Medici, P3 Motorsports, Martin Roessler, Ted 'Ferret Fotographics' Walker, and Russell Whitworth. Every attempt has been made to attribute each photograph. We apologise for any errors or omissions.

We have been very fortunate in having had access to drivers over a period of years. Special thanks go to Brian Redman, Sandro Munari, Tony Adamowicz and Jacky Ickx for sharing their thoughts about the 312P. I have to add that I also had the great fortune to drive in some of the World Championship races in 1973/74, and had the chance to be on track with the Ferrari drivers of the time. I have special memories of good times and 'close encounters' with Arturo Merzario and Carlos Pace in those days.

Ed McDonough

The 1969/1970 Ferrari 312P V-12 – The beginning

The mid-1960s saw an important change of emphasis in the way sports car racing was organised. The focus on Grand Touring cars, having become the major championship, altered, and what had been the highest category, the GT series, was no longer run after 1965. That year had seen the battles between the Ford GT40, the Shelby Daytona Coupé, Porsche 904 and Ferrari 275P2. Sebring had a class for sports-racing machines, and the race was won by the Chaparral 2A. Le Mans was taken by a Chinetti-entered 250 LM Ferrari, and Ford was seriously defeated.

In 1966 and 1967 there were two separate championships: the Trophy des Constructeurs, which would be a Prototype formula (Group 6) for cars Over 2 Litres and Under 2 Litres; and the Championnat des Voitures de Sport. This second parallel series was for cars that had been homologated, and at least 50 of which had been built. There were three displacement categories: Over 2 Litres; 1.3 to 2.0 Litres; and Up to 1.3 Litres. These were the years of the great unlimited sports racers and prototypes. Ford won the Over 2-Litre Manufacturers' title for Prototypes, and Porsche the Sports Car Championship. 1967 was not a Ferrari year and Porsche again took the larger class in the Sports Car title fight.

However, part way through 1967, the CSI, the rule-making arm of the FIA, made a decision to move away from maintaining any resemblance to road-going vehicles and announced that the 1968 championship, the International Championship of Makes, would be for 3-litre Prototypes. This totally reversed earlier trends, and the new cars would essentially be thinly-disguised F1 cars. Gone were the unlimited Chaparrals, Ford MkIIs, the Mirage and the P-series Ferraris. It was later declared that Group 4 cars, of which 50 had been homologated, would be allowed to run with the Group 6 cars. Without realising it, the CSI had opened the door to the Porsche 917 and Ferrari 512 which, in many ways, overshadowed the primary prototype series.

Enzo Ferrari's response to the new rules was to refuse to send any works cars to the 1968 races. He didn't have an engine, and said he wouldn't participate for the foreseeable future. Group 4 Ford GT40s won key races, including Le Mans, and fought all season against Porsche 907s and 908s.

Enter the Ferrari 312P

The homologation number for Group 4 cars was lowered to 25 in the hope that older cars would continue to fill the ranks. This change in numbers prompted both Porsche and Ferrari to plan new cars; Porsche in 1969, and Ferrari in 1970. However, Ferrari changed his mind, as he often did, and produced a new car to contest the prototype series for 1969 ... the Ferrari 312P.

Ferrari chose his annual press conference in December 1968 to launch the new car. Having argued against sports car racing being taken over by Grand Prix machines in disguise, the FIA and CSI had spawned the birth of a car that was just the opposite of what they had favoured for a number of years.

The 312P was very much a Grand Prix car with a slightly modified chassis and all-enveloping bodywork. Sports car rule modifications for 1969 had also meant that there was no requirement for a full windscreen or a spare wheel. Although pre-war sports cars had also often been

GP machines with more clothes, this disguise was indeed very thin. Ferrari used the V-12 3-litre engine which had been powering Chris Amon and Jacky Ickx in their 312 F1 cars throughout 1968, and would do so again in 1969 for Chris Amon and for Pedro Rodriguez when he joined the team in July. This V-12, with a 60-degree vee, had four valves per cylinder and a bore and stroke of 77 x 53.5mm, and produced in the region of 420bhp at 9800rpm. The compression was reduced from 11.8:1 to 11:1 on Lucas fuel injection. However, a new exhaust and different camshafts meant that the sports car was every bit as quick as its F1 predecessor. The V-12 was coupled directly to a 5-speed plus reverse Ferrari gearbox with single-plate clutch.

The new car was a semi-monocoque construction with the engine/gearbox connected directly to the monocoque, with a rear space-frame for the suspension at the back. It used a combination of alloy and fibreglass panels and, with a wheelbase of 2370mm, it was a low and sleek package indeed. The suspension was comprised of adjustable double wishbones, with outboard springs at the front, and the car was fitted with Girling ventilated disc brakes, 15in wheels by Campagnolo and Firestone tyres. The Firestones sat on knock-off alloy rims, 10.5in wide at the front, and 13.5in at the rear. The aerodynamic body was designed by Ing. Colibri, his first important Ferrari design, and it stood barely three feet high, so it looked not only aesthetically pleasing, but very purposeful. A number of the panels had been riveted to the chassis to add strength and stiffness, and its overall finish drew on the lessons Ferrari had learned about design in its first CanAm venture in 1968.

Sebring 12 Hours

Ferrari's original intention had been to enter all the Championship rounds, but this was dealt a blow when the first car, chassis 0868, was damaged in testing at Vallelunga, and Ferrari's season start was delayed until the Sebring 12 Hours on March 22. Only one car was entered, something which happened several times in the 1969 season, and that weakened Ferrari's chances of victory. The reality was that Ferrari was short of money in those days, the FIAT money was going principally towards the development of road cars, and that turned out to be costly when it came to fighting off the opposition.

The repaired chassis 0868 appeared at Sebring for Ferrari regular Chris Amon and Italian-American Mario Andretti. The Daytona 24 Hours had gone to the Group 4 Lola T70s, but nine 3-litre Group 6 prototypes came to Sebring. The new Alfa Romeo T33/3 had looked promising in testing by John Surtees, but when he arrived in Florida, he found Carlo Chiti had changed all the settings, and in addition his tyre contract dispute had not been settled so he walked out on the team.

Andretti made everyone stand up and take notice when he put the new Group 6 Ferrari 312P firmly on pole position. The Nanni Galli/Ignazio Giunti Alfa was next, followed by the Mitter/Schutz Porsche 908/2 as the grid lined up alongside the pits for the last ever Le Mans start at Sebring. Siffert was away and gone in his Porsche with Daytona winner Mark Donohue hot on his trail; they fought it out for the first hour. Chris Amon pulled over out on the circuit when he couldn't change gear and apparently gave the gearshift mechanism a good kick. This delicate manoeuvre seemed to do the job and he was soon off and running again. As the race approached half distance, the Ferrari had surprised all those who'd doubted its reliability and was up in second place behind the leading Mitter/Schutz 908/2. Two more Porsches and a GT40 followed. Not long after the six-hour mark, Umberto Maglioli driving in a strange, for him, Chevron B8 had the rear body section fall off, whereupon it was collected by the Amon/Andretti Ferrari. This meant a long pit stop to clear the debris, but the car continued to overheat, and ran slower, and with a lot of smoke pouring out, for the rest of the race.

Then the Porsches all started running into trouble, most of them with cracking chassis. Amazingly, Amon and Andretti pushed the 312P into the lead but they were running with almost no water in the cooling system and couldn't maintain a winning pace (the mechanics had put oil in the water radiator as it had a higher boiling point). There was also a rumour that wine had been used in that

Americans get their first look at the 312P. Chassis 0868 at Sebring in practice. (Courtesy Dave Kutz)

Chris Amon and Mario Andretti brought 0868 home in second place in its first race. (Courtesy Dave Kutz)

race for the same reason! Jacky Ickx and Jackie Oliver moved past them into the lead, the Ferrari finishing only a single lap behind in second place. The result made a Ferrari victory look realistic.

Le Mans test weekend
A second 312P was completed in time for the Le Mans test weekend at the end of March, just after Sebring. This was chassis 0870, and it was dispatched to the Sarthe

Chris Amon
New Zealander Amon began his F1 career driving Lolas and a Lotus 25 BRM for Reg Parnell in 1963 and 1964. He joined Scuderia Ferrari in 1967 for three seasons, where he had a number of good results but could never quite manage the victory that everyone thought he deserved and was inevitable. He then did a number of seasons as a Ferrari sports car driver. In 1970 Chris went to March, and then Matra, Tecno, drove his own Amon-Cosworth, and finally went to Ensign. Chris was a competent sports car and CanAm driver for a number of teams before retiring back to his native New Zealand.

Chris Amon with 1967 team manager Franco Lini. (Courtesy Ed McDonough)

Mario Andretti
Andretti moved from his native Italy in 1959 and, throughout the 1960s, achieved virtually everything possible in American racing, from winning in midget cars to winning the Indy 500. He drove, off and on, for Lotus, Ferrari, March and Parnelli, before spending a few more years with Lotus. He excelled in NASCAR, and was a regular sports car driver throughout his long career. At Ferrari he co-drove with all the team's top drivers, including Amon, Ickx and Rodriguez, and scored numerous wins.

Mario Andretti and his occasional Ferrari teammate, Pedro Rodriguez. (Courtesy Ed McDonough)

circuit for Chris Amon. Some reports have two cars there from Ferrari but only 0870 ran and it was a disappointing performance. Porsche had brought the new Group 4, 4.5-litre 917 to Le Mans. It had been rumoured that the new car had diabolical handling, and indeed it did, but it was three seconds faster than the next car, the Group 6 Matra. A Lola T70 was 3rd, a Porsche 908L 4th, and the Ferrari 312P down in 5th, a full seven seconds behind the Porsche 917. Group 4 was supposed to be slower than Group 6! It was decided fairly quickly that when the cars returned for the actual race at Le Mans, they would be in closed coupé format to improve the aerodynamics.

The Brands Hatch 6 Hours

The Brands Hatch 6-hour race took place on a cold, blustery weekend in mid-April. John Wyer entered both GT40 and Mirage-BRM models, two Ford F3Ls were there, four Porsche 908s and no fewer than eight Lola T70s, 2 Mk3s and six Mk3Bs. Ferrari had entered 0870 for Amon and Pedro Rodriguez, and 0868 was entered but did not appear.

Jo Siffert was in determined mood all weekend and put the Porsche 908/2 he was sharing with Brian Redman on pole, with Amon and Rodriguez not far off in second with a car that didn't totally suit the tighter circuit but certainly looked good in action. The co-authors of this book were there to get their first glimpse of a 312P ... the first, but not the last by any means.

Siffert's pole-sitter was having electrical dramas just before the start and the mechanics were sure it was not going to last, as it certainly didn't sound right. Amon was first into Paddock Bend, the Ferrari sounding magnificent. Siffert hung on for four laps and then went ahead. Whatever was happening in the engine compartment, Siffert was driving furiously. These two pulled away and the Lola pack started to get amongst the Porsches. Amon dropped back

Pedro Rodriguez in practice for the Brands Hatch 6 Hours in chassis 0870. (Courtesy Ed McDonough)

Pedro Rodriguez and Chris Amon discuss their car in situ! (Courtesy Peter Collins)

Rodriguez and Amon managed to get 0870 on the front row at Brands Hatch. (Courtesy Ed McDonough)

after having to make a stop for a puncture. The Lolas began having problems and it wasn't long before the Porsches had the three top spots. The Ferrari moved back up into 4th behind the German squad, with Herrmann in another 908 just behind, and the Mirage-BRM next.

Siffert's car now seemed to be running perfectly and he pulled out a huge gap of two laps on the 908 of Elford/Attwood. In wet conditions many cars spun, and virtually all the Lolas seemed to suffer from cracked suspension uprights; Bonnier having a big crash in his. Pedro Rodriguez did his bit by pushing the Ferrari past the Mitter/Schutz Porsche into 3rd. The German pair put on a fine demonstration towards the end to regain the place, making for a Porsche 1-2-3 with Amon/Rodriguez 4th, and the Group 4 Wyer GT40 of Hobbs and Hailwood 5th. The Mirage had retired, as had all but one of the Lolas. The Porsche handling was excellent on this circuit, and, while the 312P continued to impress, it was four laps down at the end of six hours.

Pedro has 0870 in 4th place near the end of the Brands Hatch race. (Courtesy Ed McDonough)

Chris Amon comes up behind the Lola T70 Mk3B of Revson/Hulme/Axelsson at Druids Bend. (Courtesy Ed McDonough)

Pedro Rodriguez

Pedro Rodriguez and his younger brother Ricardo were international sensations when they first appeared at races in 1957 and immediately challenged many of the current stars. They went to Le Mans to race together but Ricardo was turned away because of his age. Nevertheless, with the intervention of Luigi Chinetti and the North American Racing Team, they were both soon taking part in the world's most prestigious events, often leading though rarely winning. Ricardo made his F1 debut first but was killed at the 1962 Mexican Grand Prix. Pedro became one of the best sports car exponents of all time, driving for Ford, Ferrari and Porsche, winning at Le Mans in 1968.

Pedro Rodriguez about to go to work.
(Courtesy Ferret Fotographics)

Monza 1000 Kilometres

Only ten days after the Brands Hatch race, Ferrari finally sent two cars to Monza for the 1000 Kilometres. These were 0868 for Rodriguez and Peter Schetty, and 0870 for Amon and Andretti. It was a mixed entry, without John Wyer and either the Mirage or GT40, though there were two other GT40s, a new Matra 'interim' car, many Porsches, and several Alfa Romeos T33s (all the 2-litre versions from the previous year). The Ferraris were very much at home, which they should have been as they had done a fair amount of testing at Monza. This was the last time the banking was to be used for this race and it caused problems for many of the cars.

Amon and Andretti had managed pole for Ferrari, though Siffert and Redman split the Ferrari pair in second. Rodriguez was in fine form again in 3rd with his Swiss co-driver, then the next Porsche of Herrmann and Ahrens led the Servoz-Gavin/Guichet Matra 630/650. The first three took off and disappeared from the field, and were amongst the backmarkers in no time, not surprising as the slowest car was 78 seconds a lap slower than the leader. Andretti's Ferrari and Siffert's Porsche were soon swooping past slower cars on both sides with Pedro snapping at their exhausts. The Porsche 908s and the Matra formed the next group, while the Lolas all tended to fade fairly quickly in this race.

Siffert decided to slow and follow the two Ferraris, and he didn't have to wait long for things to change as Andretti made an early stop having worn out a tyre completely. Rodriguez then held the lead, and eventually he came in for his stop at the same time as Siffert. Schetty was quicker than Redman, and as the halfway point approached, Schetty held off Redman fairly easily while Andretti moved back up to 3rd. Then Schetty had a tyre go whilst leading and stopped, finding the V-12 difficult to restart. Redman now led, with Andretti on his tail. When Andretti came in for his regular stop, Amon got in but didn't make a lap as the Ferrari engine failed on lap 39. Redman then had a lap on Schetty who had to make another unscheduled halt for tyres. Pedro took over, and, in what was his customary

Rodriguez and eventual winner Siffert come up to lap the GT40 of Hanrioud/Martin at Monza. (Courtesy Ed McDonough)

Pedro Rodriguez pounds round the Monza banking before his first brush with the barriers. (Courtesy Acquati)

Peter Schetty

The Swiss driver Peter Schetty had started in hillclimbs in Switzerland in the early 1960s, and by the middle of the decade was driving Mustangs for Scuderia Filipinetti. He drove and developed the works Abarth in 1967 before being hired to drive the works Ferrari 212E in the European Mountain Climb Championship. He developed that car through 1968 and competed with it through 1969, winning every event in which he took part. He drove occasionally in other races, then became a regular in the 512 in 1970 and 1971, before becoming team manager of Ferrari's F1 and sports car teams. He returned to the family business at the end of 1972.

Peter Schetty, on the left, Ferrari team manager. (Courtesy Peter Collins)

fashion, took on the aura of a man on a mission. Catching Redman, Pedro was put off by a slow car, smacked the Armco and stopped for body repairs. He barely lost any time, though, and was soon flying. However, as he came up to go past the Herrmann/Ahrens 908, the panels which had not been fastened properly came off and Pedro slammed even harder into the barriers, this time seriously damaging the car and retiring. In the end Siffert/Redman won from Herrmann/Ahrens, with a 907 Porsche 3rd. Again, the 312P was a race leader, but there was no result for it this time.

Spa 1000 Kilometres

Ferrari decided not to waste time with the 312P at the Targa Florio, so Porsche took its third win in a row, Mitter and Schutz taking the honours.

Two cars were entered for the Spa 1000 Kilometres on May 11, the repaired 0870 for Rodriguez and Englishman David Piper, and 0868 for Andretti and Schetty. This second car did not appear and Piper was standing in for Amon who was ill. The race was most significant for the first racing appearance of Porsche's 917, two of which came for Siffert/Redman and Mitter/Schutz. Porsche also brought four long-tail 908s in coupé form.

Siffert was terrifying to watch in the new 917, needing the entire width of the straights to keep the car on the road at nearly 350kph! When asked, Siffert and Redman opted to race the 908 having set fastest time during practice in the 917. The Lola of Paul Hawkins took pole when the 917 was wheeled away. Mitter would start the other 917 from 8th spot but was relieved when the engine lasted only one lap. Ickx and Oliver had one of the Mirage-BRMs second fastest, with Siffert's 908 3rd and Rodriguez in the 312P 4th.

As the flag went down it was the quartet of Lola, Porsche, Ferrari and Mirage for the first lap around the fabulous 'old' Spa circuit. After two laps, Rodriguez tucked in tightly behind Siffert and together they shot past Hawkins and were off ... again. In just a few laps they were into the backmarkers. Karl von Wendt, who was sharing a 907 with Willy Kauhsen, was caught unawares as Siffert flashed past him on the left in the middle of Eau Rouge. Von Wendt moved over without realising Pedro was doing the same on the right and the 907 was off into the bushes in a split second. Pedro stopped for repairs to a damaged nose and Hawkins was back in second.

Pedro got second place back and was gaining on Siffert when it came time to change drivers. Piper, though very competent, hadn't been in the 312P before, so Redman pulled out a gap on him. Redman was almost a lap up when he came in to hand back to Siffert, while Piper was fending off the Elford 908. When Pedro got back in behind the wheel, it was again 'mission time.' Siffert tried to lap

Rodriguez about to qualify 0870 at Spa. (Courtesy Ferrari)

The Ferrari 312P (#8) at the start behind the JW Mirage. (Courtesy Ed McDonough)

David Piper

English driver David Piper was racing seriously in the early 1950s, and has had an almost continuous history of competition until the present time. He raced Lotus sports cars with success internationally, and by 1958 was a full-time professional driver. He went to the Tasman series in 1960, finishing 2nd to Jack Brabham in the Wigram Trophy. He raced a Ferrari 250 GTO from 1962, and won the Kyalami Nine Hours on five occasions. He was an occasional Ferrari works driver, did Le Mans several times, and was a respected endurance driver in Ferraris and Lolas.

David Piper, right, after finishing 2nd at Spa with Rodriguez in 1969. (Courtesy Ferret Fotographic)

Nürburgring 1000 Kilometres

Three weeks after Spa the teams journeyed to Germany for the Nürburgring 1000 Kilometres. Again, Ferrari sent a single car, 0870, for Amon and Rodriguez. This race made it very clear that Ferrari might have done much better in 1969 if it had taken the trouble to prepare two good cars for races. Porsche on the other hand, was struggling with its own overkill policy, though strength in numbers ensured a win. Porsche brought eight 908s in closed and open form in addition to the 917. This was to be driven by BMW regulars Quester and Hahne, but when BMW found out it said 'no!' in no uncertain terms. Frank Gardner and David Piper were drafted in to drive the 917, and Frank still tells stories about the reason they got the drive: "They must have thought we were the stupidest!" Piper managed tenth fastest but the car was still a nightmare.

Siffert managed fastest time in practice, but Pedro didn't hold back and was only a tenth of a second slower in the 312P over the 14-mile circuit. Then came six Porsches and the Mirage of Ickx, now with a Cosworth V-8 replacing the BRM engine. Juan Fangio was the official starter on the rolling start (the Le Mans start was now gone) and when the flag was a bit hesitant in coming down, Mitter jumped into the lead while Siffert and Amon were trying to work out what was happening. Siffert got back in front by the end of the opening lap. Amon had been swamped by the 908s and had gone to the back of that pack, but soon worked his way to 3rd. The 312P was lifting in spectacular fashion over the many humps at the 'Ring but, on the whole, was handling very well.

Rain showers visited several parts of the circuit, catching out the drivers (Masten Gregory was in a field in his 910 trying to find a way out, and Teddy Pilette was stuck on a guard rail in the VDS Alfa Tipo 33 with the 2.5-litre engine). Amon seemed to be the most competent driver in the difficult conditions, and the 312P was coping with both dry and wet roads, moving back up to second spot. He was beginning to catch Siffert, and a battle for the lead looked imminent. In contrast, Gardner was struggling in 14th in the 917. Amidst all the Porsches coming in at once for their

him and drag Elford past the Ferrari as well, but Pedro wouldn't have it and held onto second to the end. Yet again, the Ferrari 312P was there or thereabouts, but Porsche had the advantage.

Rodriguez at the Nürburgring with 0870, which failed to finish. (Courtesy J Sloniger)

Amon takes over from Rodriguez for the final stint at the Nürburgring. (Courtesy J Sloniger)

changeover, the Ferrari started having trouble with clutch pressure, and Amon's last lap was slow as he pumped up the pressure so Pedro could get it out of the pit lane again. After the changes, Redman, in for Siffert, was just holding off the flying (literally) Rodriguez.

At the second stop, Amon was back in for new tyres, and he lost places to the Porsches. He started to take twenty seconds a lap off the leaders, though, setting a new lap record in the process. However, the car was vibrating under braking and then an ignition wire came off and Amon was stuck out on the circuit, with another two hours to go! Five Porsche 908s took the first five places ahead of the Kelleners/Joest GT40, the 2-litre Alfa T-33 and the 917 in 8th. Siffert and Redman had a well-deserved victory, but again the Ferrari had threatened them seriously, on a circuit where, perhaps, it shouldn't have.

Le Mans 24 Hours

The Nürburgring race was followed two weeks later by the Le Mans 24 Hours. After Le Mans there would be only two more Championship events, at Watkins Glen and the Österreichring, and the season would be over. Porsche had a healthy lead in all the major divisions of the Championship and there seemed very little chance of anyone overtaking it.

The running of the 24-hour race in 1969 had been affected by a number of unfortunate events. Alfa's Lucien Bianchi had been killed in the April tests in the new 3-litre T33, and the whole Mulsanne Straight was now lined with barriers and there were new runoff areas. F1 had been having numerous crashes due to the failure of aerodynamic devices which had developed over the last year. These were banned in both Grand Prix racing and in sports cars. Porsche was allowed to keep the movable flaps on the 917 but not on the 908. As a direct result of Bianchi's accident, Alfa didn't send any works cars so only two VDS cars from Belgium came.

Porsche brought two 917s for Elford/Attwood and Stommeln/Ahrens while Briton John Woolfe had bought the first customer car for himself and Digby Martland. Martland didn't like it and it was taken over by Herbert Linge. There were four 908s, one open car and three coupés, and the winner was very much expected to be from this quartet. Ferrari had decided after the April tests that it would build aerodynamic coupé bodies for 0868 and 0870, and these were beautiful cars; very smooth with good air penetration characteristics. However, they were still a good bit heavier than the Porsches. The intention was that these cars would be sold on to Chinetti's NART team towards the end of the season. They were to be driven at Le Mans by Amon/Schetty and Rodriguez/Piper. It would appear that the car that arrived at Le Mans as 0868 was, in fact, 0872, a new car which had been constructed as a berlinetta, not a conversion from the open car. There was also an entry for Herbert Muller and Jonathan Williams in a 312P, but this never materialised.

Matra was making a serious attempt at Le Mans this year following the potential seen in 1968 when the coupé ran in second place for a good many hours. Matra had four cars, an indication of how serious it was taking sports car racing. Servoz-Gavin had been second fastest to the 917 in April, and after a testing crash, the 650 had been reworked, with much effort going into the reliability of the V-12. The French also had eight various Alpines to cheer, all with some degree of factory support. There was no JW Mirage, but the team had its 'old' GT40s there, and there were other ageing GT40s as well, which no-one took seriously.

The two works 917s were quickest in practice, and John Woolfe's private car was 9th. 908s were 3rd and 4th, and Rodriguez/Piper were 5th, a 908 6th, and Amon 7th, so the Ferraris at least looked set for a good run. The V-12 engine had proved quite reliable for an essentially F1 unit, and it was fairly efficient in fuel terms as well.

Jacky Ickx had announced that the Le Mans start was outdated and, as other drivers ran, he walked to his GT40 and set off last. He might have been quite pleased not to be near the front, as his 13th grid position would have had him, for the first lap turned into chaos. John Woolfe desperately wanted to lead the field down the Mulsanne and he was barely in control. He hadn't bothered to do up his seat belts and, as he headed into Maison Blanche, he got two wheels off the road, lost it, rolled and the car broke in two and burned. He was thrown out and died on the way to hospital. Amon ran over the fuel tank and 0868 (or 0872) was damaged though Amon got clear. There were some photos taken at the time that showed the car wasn't 'written off' as some have said. The remains were taken back to Italy, and some of the parts plus possibly parts from the 'real' 0868, later went to Pininfarina who built a show car, the 512 Speciale, with another engine, and this is now in Belgian ownership.

Several cars had run over debris and pitted, some later retiring due to the damage. Rodriguez was in the large group which had been severely delayed by the blocked track. One of the 917s was in trouble from the beginning and the Siffert/Redman 908 retired during the 4th hour. It was at this point that the Rodriguez/Piper 312P started having minor gearbox problems which brought them into the pits. Pedro had gotten back into the lead group but though the car went on for a total of 223 laps, the gearbox got worse and worse and they had to retire.

With only a few hours to go, it looked like Porsche was going to take its first overall win at Le Mans. Elford and Attwood were doing a superb job with the surviving 917 Group 4 car and 908s were backing it up. The car started going off-song, however, and Elford and Attwood began visiting the pits. Kauhsen was now in the 2nd place 908 and suddenly found himself in the lead, and then just as suddenly found himself stopped with no clutch. Now the 1968-winning GT40 of Ickx/Oliver was in front of Herrmann and Larrousse in the 908 which was catching the Ford. In the most famous ever Le Mans finish, the Ford got there first by a few feet and Porsche was dumbstruck by the defeat.

Bridgehampton CanAm race

As neither Ferrari itself nor NART decided to enter either Watkins Glen in July or the Austrian race in August, the next appearance for a 312P would be in September for the CanAm race at Bridgehampton.

Pedro Rodriguez had competed in many races for Chinetti's team, and really got his international start driving for the New York-based team. The race on the far northern end of Long Island was the seventh round of the CanAm series, and 0870, still in coupé form, was the only new entry for the series, and thus garnered much attention. The 3-litre engine was thought unlikely to get anywhere near the much bigger American-powered machinery, but that tended to discount Pedro's determination and skill.

Bruce McLaren and Denny Hulme had so dominated the first qualifying session in their McLaren M8Bs that they went off water skiing for the next session. Chris Amon was next in the Ferrari 612P, chassis 0866, which he had been using in CanAm, and he had a hard fight with Surtees to line

0870 in coupé form at the Bridgehampton CanAm race. (Courtesy Ed McDonough)

Rodriguez at speed through the sand dunes at Bridgehampton. (Courtesy Paul Medici)

up just behind McLaren. Surtees was in a McLaren M12 for the occasion. Pedro was in 11th spot, two rows behind the Porsche 917PA of Jo Siffert. The 917 was on the verge of becoming a mighty force in both CanAm and endurance racing.

Bruce McLaren was in a state in the race morning warm-up when he thundered into the pits thinking a piston was gone. It was a rocker stud, and this was repaired. While McLaren and Hulme went off into the lead, Surtees had his engine start to overheat and he dropped back, while Amon had a rod break in the six-litre Ferrari. Siffert began to run out of fuel near the end but managed to make it into third, followed by Lothar Motschenbacher in his M12, and then the 312P of Rodriguez, with another 3-litre behind him. That was Tony Dean's 908 which did so well in the CanAm series. Chris Amon would reappear at Riverside in October with the car as the 712P, and in Texas in November as the 612P.

On the world stage, when the championships were all settled, Porsche had won the Manufacturers' Championship from Ford, Lola and Ferrari, the Grand Touring Trophy from Chevrolet and Ferrari, the Challenge Mondiale from Ford and Alfa Romeo, and the Marques Standard Points by over 100 points from Ford. With the development of the 917 continuing, 1970 didn't look much more promising for the opposition.

Specifications 1969 312P – V-12

Type	Sports Prototype Group 6
Seats	Two
Engine	Mid-engine V-12
Cylinders	12in vee at 60 degrees
Valves	48
Bore and stroke	77 x 53.5mm
Capacity	2989.5cc
Compression	11 to 1
Horsepower	420bhp @ 9800rpm
Fuel injection	Lucas indirect system
Ignition	Marelli, Marelli 10mm sparkplugs
Transmission	5-speed + reverse
Suspension	Independent on all 4 wheels; coil springs/damper units
Wheelbase	2370mm
Track	Front: 1465mm; Rear: 1500mm
Height	890mm
Weight	680kg
Tyres	Firestone – Front: 4.75/10.30 15in; Rear: 6.00/13.50 x 15in

1970 – No works Ferraris

Ferrari continued its intensive programme to improve its Grand Prix results, while at the same time embarking on the all-new 512S to compete directly with Porsche and the Porsche 917 in Group 4. Although the FIA knew that Ferrari hadn't completed the mandatory 25 cars for homologation, the go ahead was given and the cars were ready for the early season races. The 312Ps had been pensioned off to NART, who'd had 0870 and 0872 for some months, both still in coupé form.

1970 was truly to be the year of Porsche vs. Ferrari. The 917 was a better car than the 512S, though not by much. There was a great expectation that the two remaining seasons of Group 4 at this level could produce some fantastic races. The reality wasn't quite as great as the anticipation, but anyone who saw the 917s fighting the 512S never forgot the spectacle, helped along by the film initiated by Steve McQueen ... *Le Mans*.

Daytona 24 Hours

The first race came at Daytona for the 24 Hours at the end of January, and both Porsche and Ferrari sent the Group 4, 5-litre cars. The Ferrari numbers were swelled by the two Chinetti NART 312Ps, with 0870 for Tony Adamowicz and David Piper and 0872 for Sam Posey and Mike Parkes. The manufacturers of 3-litre cars were very disappointed by the way attention had switched to the Group 4 cars from the prototypes, and Alfa Romeo and Matra were really biding their time until the next rule change in 1972. Some of the privateers and smaller teams soldiered on with cars that were not competitive for outright victory but were nevertheless still in the running for good results.

The general feeling during the early practice sessions was that the Daytona track favoured the 917 and 512S, and that was where the main battle would be. In Group 6, for the prototypes, only one of the Porsche 908s survived practice as the Porsche team was concentrating its efforts on the 917, and the older 908s got less attention. The new Matra 650 looked like it might well give a good account of itself. Andretti, Merzario and Ickx put their 512S on pole from the Siffert/Redman and Rodriguez/Kinnunen 917s, with the Elford/Ahrens Porsche Salzburg 917 next ahead of the Ickx/Schetty 512S. Most of the main teams had now taken to having their drivers doing a stint in each car. Sam Posey and Mike Parkes in 0872 were 9th quickest, seven seconds off pole, while the second 312P was 13th, four seconds slower; but then, this was a 24-hour race ...

When the race started it was an immediate confrontation between the big Porsches and Ferraris with the two Gulf 917s going in front to take the lead, spearheaded by Pedro Rodriguez who had now left Ferrari to join Jo Siffert as the best pair of sports car drivers of the period. After the first stops, which came earlier for the thirsty Ferrari 512Ss than the 917s, Redman was in front but had a brake pipe sever and lost time. Rodriguez went in front and was never headed. The Matra had to have a replacement distributor fitted by Pescarolo on the circuit and dropped well down. At midnight the two 312Ps were running smoothly in 6th and 7th. Posey and Parkes were forced to change a radiator. As morning dawned, the Gulf 917 led with its teammate 2nd, until the clutch went on the latter and Andretti moved the 512S into 2nd. Parkes and Posey were in 3rd with the other 312P in 6th.

The Posey/Parkes 0872 in the paddock at the start of the weekend. Note the boy in the background sitting on the alloy wings of a Ferrari 275 GTB! (Courtesy Fred Lewis)

The front end of 0872 gets a thorough check before practice. (Courtesy Fred Lewis)

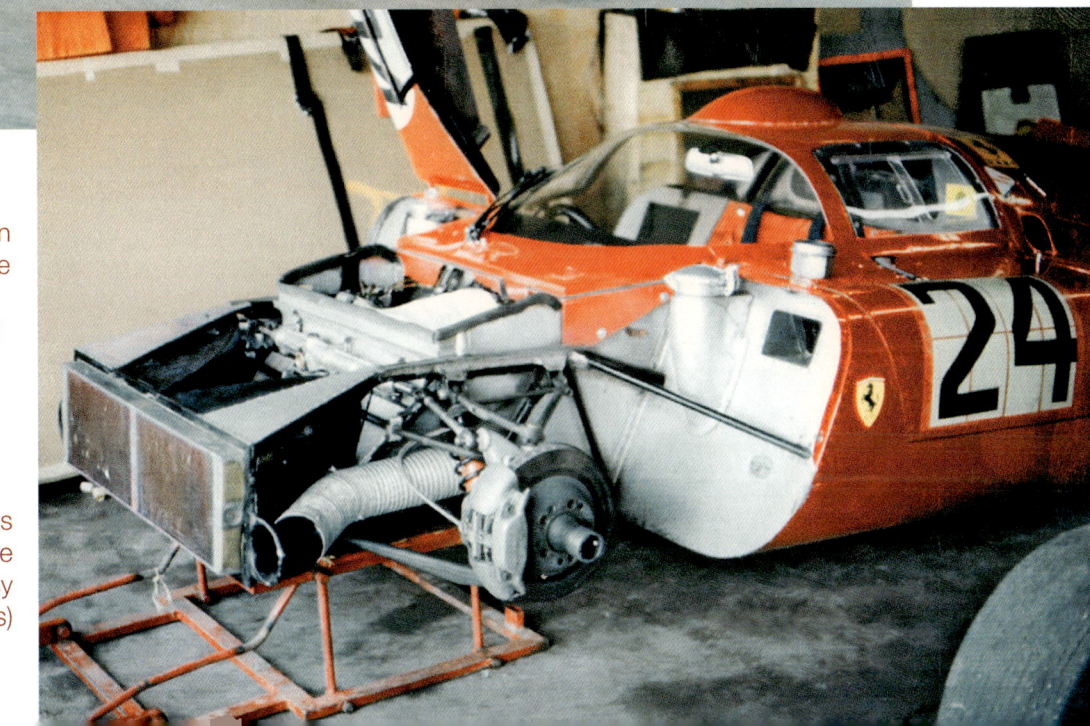

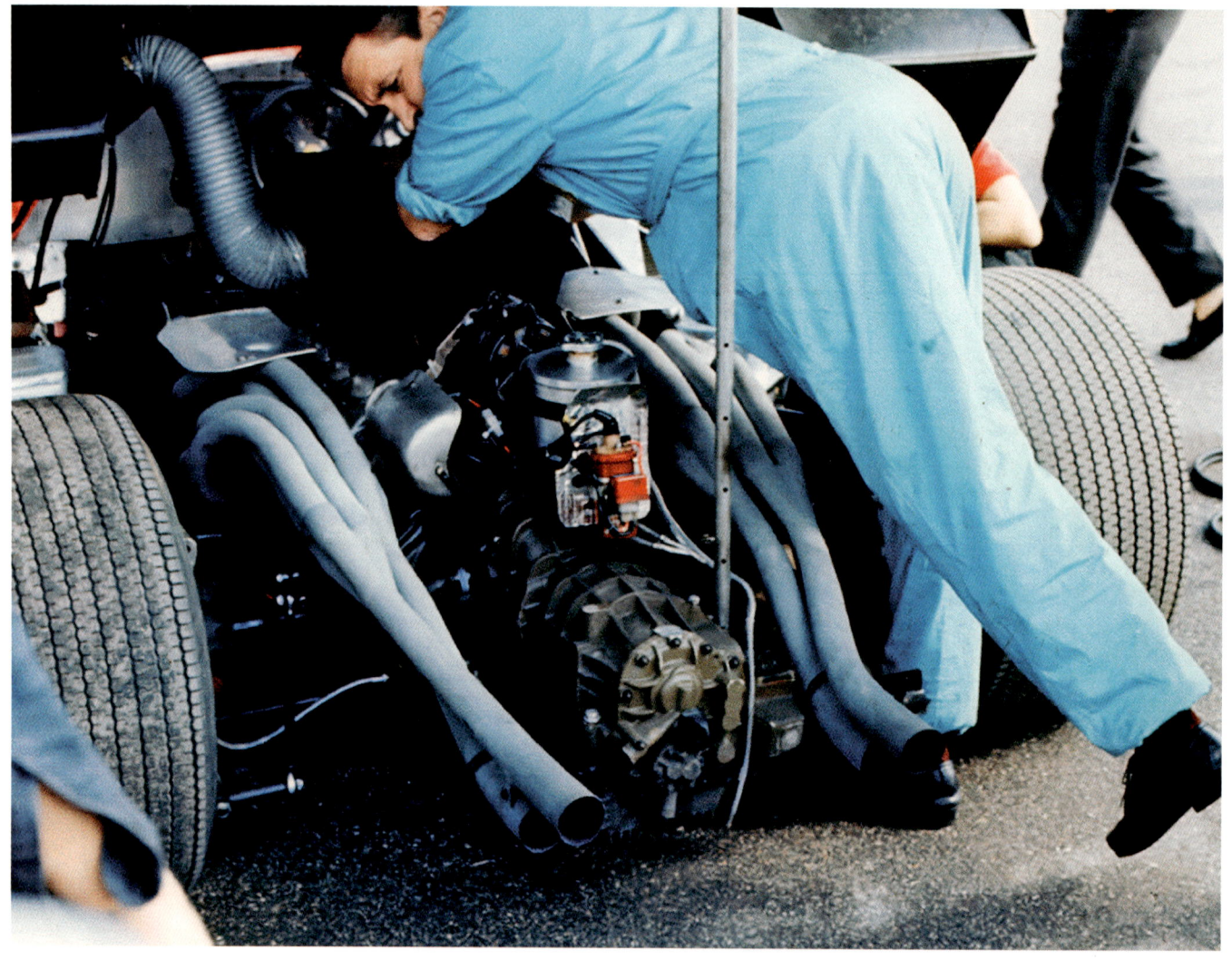

A view of the V-12 engine in the Adamowicz/Piper car, 0870, before the action starts at Daytona. (Courtesy Fred Lewis)

After 24 long hours, the Gulf cars managed to take the first two positions from the 512S, with Posey and Parkes 4th winning the Prototype class, and their teammates Adamowicz and Piper in 5th. As in 1969, Ferrari could be optimistic, but would it ever beat the Porsches?

Opposite top: Posey/Parkes in the early stages of the 24 Hours. They came 4th. (Courtesy Fred Lewis)

Opposite: The beautiful lines of 0870 are revealed in this shot of the car at speed. (Courtesy Fred Lewis)

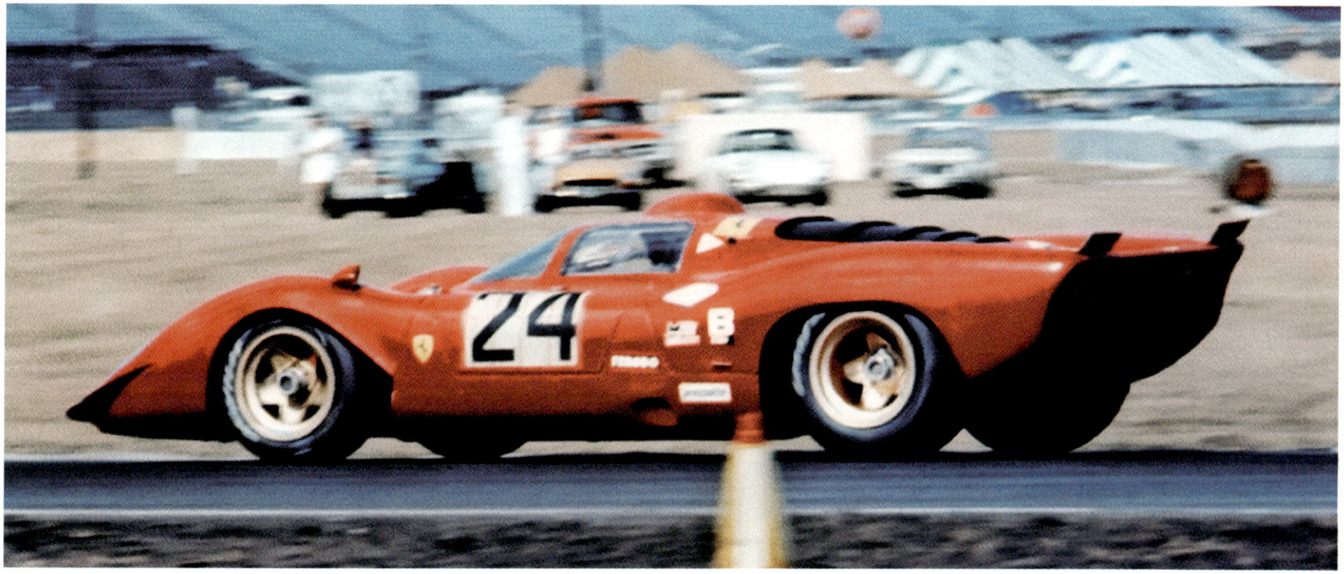
24

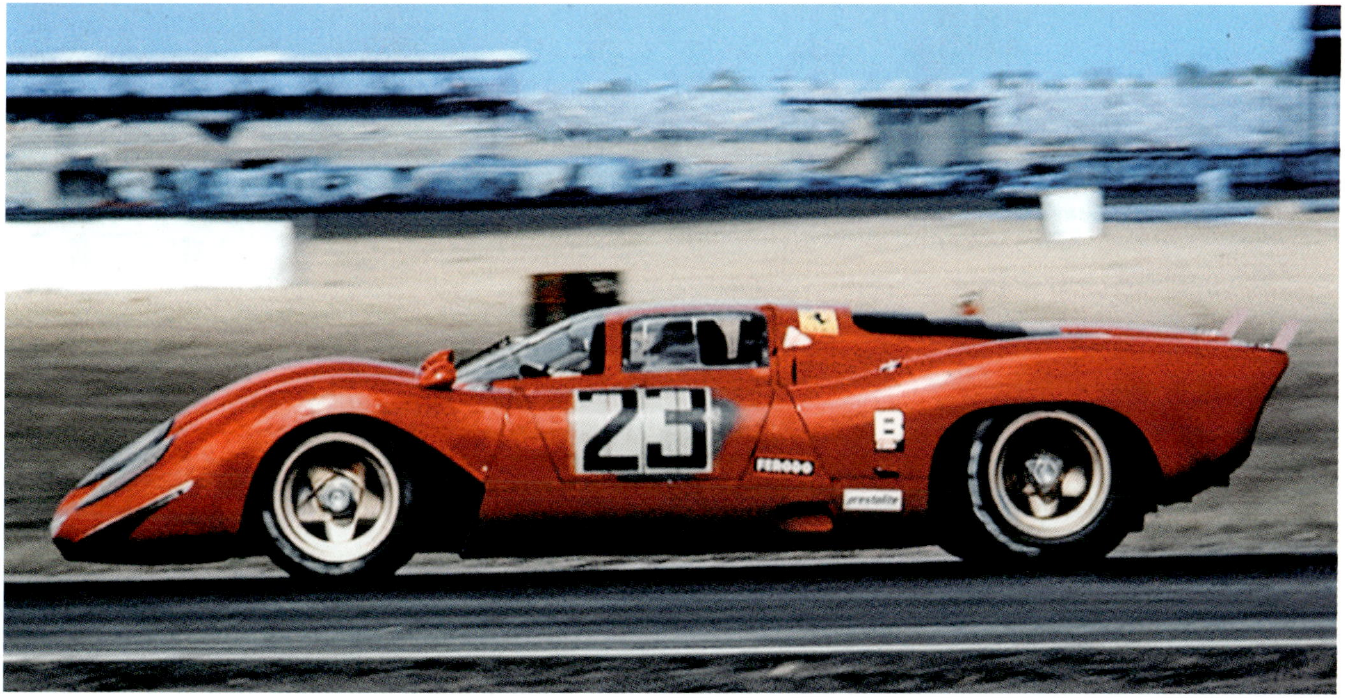
23
FERODO

Sam Posey

This genial, well educated American grew up and raced at Lime Rock Park, near his Sharon, Connecticut home. He worked his way quickly through the ranks of US club racing, won some Formula A events, and began to feature in TransAm racing, as well as getting the occasional Indy car drive on road circuits. He had several Ferrari sports car drives, notably at Daytona and Le Mans.

Mike Parkes

Parkes had been a regular driver for Ferrari in the early and mid-1960s, and he returned to the team in 1970 after not having raced for some time due to a serious accident. He'd made his race debut in 1952, and was very competitive in GT cars, beating Stirling Moss at Goodwood in 1961. This got him a works drive at Le Mans where he was second with Mairesse. He made his F1 debut at the French Grand Prix in 1966, coming second. However, his crash at Spa that year led to his becoming a development driver for Ferrari, but he had a gradual return to racing in 1969. He was widely regarded as somewhat arrogant in his manner.

Tony Adamowicz

Tony 'A to Z', as he is known, has a career going back to the early 1960s. He was a regional champion and then was a serious competitor in TransAm racing before getting behind the wheel of several sports cars in endurance races. He is one of the very few drivers ever to race both the Ferrari 512 and the Porsche 917. He had good performances at Daytona and Le Mans in the early 1970s, and then ventured into CanAm. He remains a very active participant on the motor racing scene in the USA.

Sam Posey.
(Courtesy Casey Annis)

Mike Parkes.
(Courtesy Pete Austin)

Tony Adamowicz.
(Courtesy Casey Annis)

Sebring 12 Hours

Nearly two months went by before the next race was due, the Sebring 12 Hours, where the 312P had made its debut the previous year. This time all the attention – which wasn't focussed on the presence of Steve McQueen and his Porsche 908 preparing for the film *Le Mans* – was on the upcoming struggle between four Porsche 917s and a batch of open and closed Ferrari 512S contenders. The NART entry for the Prototype Group 6 312Ps took a back seat for the most part.

0870 was down for Adamowicz and Luigi 'Coco' Chinetti Jr to drive, while 0872 would be in the hands of Parkes and American Chuck Parsons. A third 312P was listed in the original entry, but this car did not actually exist so it was a not surprising absentee.

Tony Adamowicz and Luigi Chinetti Jr were driving 0870 at Sebring. (Courtesy Lou Galanos)

The race had a very strong entry as, on top of all the Porsches and Ferraris, there were Lolas, Ford GT40s, Chevrons and Abarths. Alfa Romeo made a return visit to Florida with the new, squarer-shaped T33/3 which had been going very well in testing and practice. Matra was also there with a car for Dan Gurney, to be shared with Francois Cevert, as well as the other machine for Pescarolo/Servoz-Gavin.

Practice and qualifying saw the 512S of Andretti/Merzario on pole from the Siffert/Redman/Kinnunen 917 Gulf car, the Elford/Ahrens Salzburg 917, Ickx and Schetty's 512S, and the Rodriguez/Kinnunen/Siffert Gulf 917. Only one of these five cars would make it into the top ten at the finish. Parkes and Parsons qualified 0872 in 14th and 0870 managed 16th, which wasn't particularly promising, though all were clear that Sebring is very hard on brakes and gearboxes. The Steve McQueen/Peter Revson 908 was one spot in front of 0870 on the grid.

Mario Andretti timed the rolling start to perfection and the 512S led away, and though Siffert momentarily forced his way by, Mario took back the lead and held it until the first regular pit stop. Porsche did a much better job of getting its cars in and out of the pits than Ferrari, and after all the changes had been made, Porsche had the first four places ahead of the Ickx/Schetty 512S, and the Matra led the Group 6 field. A number of 'comings together' at the Hairpin, however, and the two Salzburg 917s were gone, as was Posey's 512S. The two leading Gulf cars then had minor troubles and, just after three hours, Ferraris were 1-2-3, while the Alfas were much slower than they had been in practice.

At halfway, Parkes and Parsons were behind the McQueen 908 which was trailing the three 512S leaders. The 512S train started to separate and Andretti and Merzario still led but the other cars were faltering. With only two hours to go, Andretti was well in front of McQueen, the Hezemans T33 and Siffert's 917.

Mario came in to hand over and said the gearbox was giving problems, and the next time the pit crew saw Merzario was when he came in on foot. Siffert then went to

In the early laps 0872 runs behind the works Alfas and alongside the McQueen/Revson Porsche 908. (Courtesy Lou Galanos)

The McQueen/Revson Porsche goes inside 0870. (Courtesy Lou Galanos)

Chuck Parsons brakes 0872 for the hairpin at Sebring. (Courtesy Dave Kutz)

A very typical scene at the old Sebring airfield circuit. (Courtesy Lou Galanos)

the front and Andretti was moved into the Giunti/Vaccarella 512S. 0870 had retired due to overheating back on lap 56. With only 55 minutes left, Andretti was driving the race he regarded as his best. He moved up to second and, when the Siffert/Rodriguez car had another hub failure, he was in front, though very low on fuel. Andretti stopped for some fuel with two laps to go and went out as the Revson/McQueen 908 came out of the final corner, Andretti making it to the finish just ahead of the Porsche. The Hezemans/Gregory Alfa was third, Rodriguez/Siffert/Kinnunen 4th, the Matra 5th, and 6th was 0872 of Parkes and Parsons, a reasonable finish for them though they were only fourth in Group 6.

Luigi Chinetti Jr

'Coco,' as he was sometimes known, was, of course, the son of the famed ex-Le Mans winner and long-time Ferrari importer, Luigi Sr. He was a partner in his father's business and in the North American Racing Team. In addition to gaining some fame by marrying heiress Mamie Spears Reynolds, he had access to racing and proved a competent driver while doing a number of endurance races for NART. He also had a hand in designing a NART Cadillac and has remained active on the historic motor racing scene.

Luigi Chinetti Jr
(Courtesy Peter Collins)

Le Mans 24 Hours

It was then nearly three months until the next (and last) appearance in period for these 312P cars ... well, at least in the coupé format in which they raced in 1970. Porsche 917s took the Championship races at Brands Hatch and Monza, 908s did it at the Targa Florio, the 917 was in charge at Spa, and the 908 at Nürburgring. In all of these races the Ferrari 512S put on more than a good show and was always there in the results; it just couldn't win!

Luigi Chinetti brought 0870 and 0872 to Le Mans to contest the Group 6 class and to back up his own 512S as well as the other 512 Ferraris. 0870 was to be shared by Sam Posey and Tony Adamowicz. It seems that Francois Migeault may have been down to drive this car as well. Adamowicz was in 0872, with Chuck Parsons, and this car set 28th fastest time in qualifying, while 0870 was 29th; not a bad set of times for a 24-hour event. However, there was a last minute hitch and 0870 was withdrawn as a promised sponsorship arrangement failed to materialise, which was a great shame. 0872, in spite of some problems, worked its way up to tenth at the end of a hard race. The Porsche Salzburg 917 of Attwood and Herrmann won the race from another 917, a 908 and two Ferrari 512S entries. The 908 took the Group 6 class, and Sam Posey had the good fortune to have been swapped from 0870 to the NART 512S with which he and Ronnie Bucknam finished 4th.

Tony Adamowicz commented on how the choice of car and drivers came about:

"Both the 312Ps arrived at Le Mans in 1970. The 0872 car, and the Parkes 'bubble roof' was chosen to race. I recall asking to drive 0870 because it was the one I drove at Daytona with David Piper, and because it didn't have the ugly bubble (for Mike Parkes' height). I thought the bubble car would be slower aerodynamically than 0870. Both Chuck Parsons and I were short-torsoed and could get away without the ugly bubble.

"I was never told the 0870 car was sold, only that the 0872 bubble roof car was better prepared for the race. Both cars went through scrutineering. I didn't buy that 0872

The NART-entered 0872 of Adamowicz/Parsons at Le Mans during a pit stop. It was unclassified, though ran well for some hours. (Courtesy F1Photo)

was better, because I knew it was crashed into the wall at Daytona by Parkes who fell asleep at the wheel.

"The 0872 car was far from prepared as indicated. It had terrible bump steer to the point that it was unmanageable. I had to beg them to do a chassis alignment and bump steer adjustment. The cars when driven at Daytona or Sebring did not have ill-handling. I tried to convince Chuck Parsons that the car was great. He hated it, and in the rain that

Tony Adamowicz thoroughly enjoyed his drive at Le Mans. (Courtesy Besnault)

came, allowed me to do the maximum stint allowed by the rules."

Tony Adamowicz would later describe his 1970 Le Mans experience in detail:

"It was June 1970 and I was en route from Los Angeles to Paris, France ... this was a dream come true for a kid from Port Henry, New York. Our recent success at the Daytona 24 Hours in the NART Ferrari 312P proved that the car had the strength and integrity to do the job. I was paired at Daytona with Englishman David Piper, while Ferrari engineer Mike Parkes was with Sam Posey in the other twin 312P. The Luigi Chinetti NART team came in 4th and 5th overall, and 1st and 2nd in class. My co-driver for Le Mans would be Chuck Parsons of CanAm fame and a successful long distance driver as well. I was anxious to have Chuck share some of his experiences at Le Mans, since he had driven a Ferrari 365 P2 back in 1967.

"Upon landing in Paris I picked up a rental car and headed for Sarthe. After checking in at the hotel, I headed a few miles south to the circuit. The circuit was closed and the first practice would not be until the following afternoon. I took the opportunity to drive around parts of the track that were public roads and walked the sections between White House and Tertre Rouge that were reserved for racing only.

"On my walk I couldn't help but notice that there were

numerous plaques with crosses along the edge of the track – marking spots where both drivers and spectators had lost their lives. The first such memorial I came upon was in the Dunlop bend where Walt Hansgen, one of my mentors, had been killed in a Ford GT40 in testing in 1966. My sobering tour of the circuit left me anxious to return to the hotel to meet up with my co-driver, Chuck.

"The next two days of practice and qualifying gave me ample time to learn the circuit and get comfortable with the 312P. There was a virtual armada of Ferrari 512s and Porsche 917s, all in long-tail configuration, in the field. Our chance for an overall win seemed very remote considering the titans entered; however, a victory in the 3-litre class was a good possibility with our main competition coming only from the 3-litre Porsche 908s. During practice, one of the Martini 908s collided with Jack Brabham's Matra 650, which resulted in the Porsche being totalled. So for the race it would come down to two Porsche 908s versus our lone Ferrari 312P.

"Race day, Saturday morning and dark clouds hung over the circuit and gave us a premonition of what was to come; however, we had no idea of the amount of rain we would encounter over the next 24 hours. We had qualified 25th in a field of 51 cars, and Chuck was assigned to start. The start of that year's race was unique in that it was the first to eliminate the famous 'dash across the track.' The Le Mans start had been abandoned for safety reasons and instead all drivers were strapped into their cars, which were lined up at an angle along the pit road. As the large circuit clock ticked away the final seconds, there was a brief moment of silence, then the starter's flag dropped, and there was a cacophony of sound as the engines fired in unison, and a massive cloud of dust and exhaust fumes were left as the field shot away.

"Chuck pitted after an uneventful one hour for fuel and I slipped behind the wheel of the 312P and was soon circulating around the 8.5-mile circuit at a steady pace. The car was running perfectly and I was thoroughly enjoying the experience, when suddenly the heavens opened up around dusk and the rain began to pelt down with an intensity I had never seen before. Unfortunately, while our coupé was very well suited to the high speed Le Mans circuit, watertight it was not. The air scoops near the base of the windshield, designed to cool the various radiators and driver, now funnelled water directly into the cockpit. Soon, I was totally soaked to the skin – the blinding rain after an hour began to fill the interior with water sloshing back and forth. The effects of acceleration, braking and cornering created waves of water lapping around the foot pedals and the driver's seat. I pitted for my scheduled stop and pointed out the problem to the crew, who immediately set about drilling holes in the floor to allow for drainage!

"After handing over the next stint to Chuck, a new problem arose – the heat from the engine and front radiator had now turned the cockpit into a damp sauna. The windshield continuously fogged up and it became a dance to keep one hand on the steering wheel while the other tried to keep the screen clear. It was a struggle for Chuck and eventually he pitted for my stint. I resorted to an old remedy I had used many times in the past. The crew brought a raw potato from the food stands directly behind the pits, and I immediately sliced it in half and started rubbing the inside of the windshield while the car was being refuelled. This helped considerably. However, the relentless downpour continued through the night and began to affect the electrical system. From time to time the engine would miss or the lights would flicker. During the short pit stops, the crew would try to waterproof electrical components with WD-40 lubricant; and we kept going, hoping for, at best, a break in the weather. Between the rain and the electrical problems, along with the fogged windscreen, we were having a tough go. Many of our competitors were also having problems, and the foul weather caused a number of crashes. At the end of the 4th hour we had moved up ten places to 15th, and by midnight we were in 11th overall.

"In the night I had a big near-miss with three 360-degree spins under the Dunlop Bridge. I got the car restarted. The following lap I came in and the crew replaced a slightly damaged tail section with a spare. Steve McQueen was on hand and indicated that the camera car being used for the filming of the movie *Le Mans* didn't catch my spin and would I mind doing a retake? Now safely in the pits, I could only take humor at his suggestion.

"When the sun finally rose Sunday morning, we were up to 8th place overall. The incessant rain finally stopped and we gained two additional places by noon. Then the electrics began to act up and we dropped back first to 9th and then 10th place. I was behind the wheel at the finish and when the flag finally dropped we were required to make one additional lap around the circuit. As I came around Indianapolis corner the engine began to misfire badly and between Arnage and White House, it finally gave up the ghost. We had come so far only to break down on the cool-off lap! I looked over at the battery mounted inside the cockpit and the terminals were smouldering. I knew then that it was not the engine but the electrics that had given up. The spectators gathered around the car and pushed it back to the pits, where an informal victory wreath was handed over and my co-driver was carrying a huge magnum of champagne. What an incredible first Le Mans it had been!"

0870 was immediately sold to Pierre Bardinon in France and it has remained in his collection. 0872, on the other hand, was returned to the USA and was modified, losing some weight, and it was then rebodied with a 'spider' body by Wayne Sparling. This was not very attractive, especially compared to how good looking the coupé had been, but it carried on racing, as we shall read in the next chapters.

1971 – 312P Ferrari flat-12 – The life of a 312P

The authors have always been inclined to think that there were three post-war periods for great sports cars. The first was in the 1950s when the early post-war production sports cars – the Jaguar C-Type and D-Type, the Ferrari Testa Rossa, and the Porsche RSK – were beginning to turn into racing prototypes. The second period was the late 1960s and early 1970s when particularly Le Mans was transformed by the Ferrari 512S and 512M, and the Porsche 917. Finally, there was the period which immediately followed these 5-litre machines – the three-litre prototypes of the early to mid-1970s – the Ferrari 312P, the Matra, Alfa Romeo Tipo 33; all thinly-disguised Grand Prix cars.

Many fans found the battles between the Porsche 917 and the Ferrari 512 in 1970 the most exciting of the post-war period, and if you weren't around in the 1950s and 1960s, it would be easy to believe that was the case. I remember during that time that there was continual discussion about the five-litre cars being too fast, and it was clear that it would not be long before the size of the current three-litre formula for Grand Prix cars would influence what was going on in sports car racing, and eventually affect the regulations. Then the new regulations which defined the World Manufacturers' Championship came into effect from 1972, and the big cars were going to be dead. But the 5-litre machines would run again in 1971, which gave Ferrari time to think about what to do after the 512.

Enzo Ferrari and his team, particularly Mauro Forghieri, had been able to see what was coming, and work was well advanced for the new sports car formula for 1972. Ferrari and other manufacturers already had experience with smaller engines. Sports car rules were complex and there had been classes for Sports, GT, and Prototype cars for some years, and these had been the Group 4, 5 and 6 cars. However, what Ferrari was doing in 1971 was just preparation for the new rules in 1972. All the bigger 512S and 512Ms went to private teams while the factory concentrated on developing the new car.

However, the 312P was not new. As we have already seen, there had been a 312P since 1969, but these had all been using the well-known V-12 engine and ran in the Prototype class. In 1971, Mauro Forghieri came up with a new idea for sports cars; the use of his new flat-12 boxer engine, which had the layout on a single plane rather than in the more traditional vee for the cylinder head. This engine had become the heart of the new Grand Prix car, and the sports prototype car used much of the same suspension. The sports car had a new two-piece fibreglass body on which was tried several different tail modifications depending on which circuit the cars were racing at. The body had a distinctive wedge shape, which was characteristic of cars throughout the 1970s.

312P or PB?

There was, and is, a problem in the way these particular cars are known; a great deal of inaccurate information exists about them. Many of the 3-litre sports cars from 1971-1972 were referred to, in later years, as the 312PB, based on the idea that the 'B' referred to 'Boxer,' the type of engine. However, according to Ferrari records, PB refers only to the 1972-updated version of the car built in 1971. The 'B' in Ferrari language refers to a Series B car rather than the Boxer engine.

The term PB originally came from journalists to distinguish it from the V-12, but even Mauro Forghieri created some confusion when he referred to his new engine as a "180-degree V-12." Really, the 312P cars continued from 1969 through 1971 in spite of the engine change to the boxer layout and the term PB shouldn't be used until 1972. Wimpffen, in *Time and Two Seats*, disagrees, and lists chassis 0878 as a PB during 1971. Antoine Prunet attempts to clarify this by saying that Ferrari had developed a 312P Boxer and that the term came from journalists. While this is important historically, it is just a relatively minor error. In fact, it might be said that chassis 0878, which we will look at very closely, turned from a 312P into a 312PB because it actually had two identities. There is an argument that the later car should have more correctly been called the 312BP, but Enzo Ferrari is said to have exclaimed: "How can I call it BP when we are contracted to Shell?" We believe that is very likely an apocryphal tale. Whatever the terminology used, this is an important car, as you will see.

Buenos Aires 1000 Kilometres

To get back to the story, it's important to note that, at the beginning of 1971, Ferrari built only one 312P. This car had chassis number 0874 and it featured the new boxer engine. It made a surprisingly quick debut at the 1971 Buenos Aires 1000 Km in Argentina where Arturo Merzario and Ignazio Giunti put it second on the grid, amongst the very fast 5-litre cars.

The start of the 1971 season saw the return of the 917 Porsches, the JW cars being pretty much as they had been in 1970. There were four works 917s and three private cars. One of these was taken over by Emerson Fittipaldi, who was about to make his debut for Alfa Romeo. The debut lasted only a few laps as he had a huge crash, which he still remembers well. In Group 6 there was a new Matra MS660, three Alfa T33s (reduced to two in pre-race practice), and there was also a 908 and an unusual McLaren 8C with a Cosworth DFV engine.

But the attention was all on the new Ferrari, which looked and sounded very effective indeed. While Rodriguez and Jackie Oliver got the 917K onto pole position, and their other team car driven by Siffert and Bell was third, the little Ferrari was just a touch slower than the fastest 917. Ignazio Giunti was an extremely quick and daring driver and he put the new car into a very competitive slot. The Elford/Larrousse 917 was 4th and Pescarolo and De Adamich got one of the Alfa T33/3s in 5th and were fairly happy with their car.

At the start Giunti made a superb start and took off in the lead, and it took a few laps before Pedro Rodriguez used the power of the 917 to get by on the straight. The Siffert and Elford cars did the same, though Siffert soon stopped to have oil cleaned from his windscreen. After ten laps Rodriguez, Elford and Giunti had pulled out a gap on the other cars. When the pit stops for the larger 5-litre cars started, Giunti had re-established himself in the lead. Beltoise in the Matra had moved up into second place but the car started to run out of fuel. It stopped altogether some 600 meters before the pit entrance and Beltoise got out and pushed the car, which of course he was not supposed to do. At the bend just before the pits he pushed it across the road.

Then Mike Parkes appeared in the 512S with Giunti tucked in close behind him. Giunti decided to pull out and shoot by Parkes, and suddenly found the nearly stationary Matra in his path. Giunti slammed into the French car and the 312P didn't stop until it was in front of the pits, burning furiously. Giunti was dead within a few minutes, though Beltoise had jumped clear just before the impact. Beltoise took most of the blame though after a long investigation, it was decided that although yellow flags were waving in warning, the marshals should have taken much stronger action to stop Beltoise, who did share some of the responsibility. It was also declared that Giunti had not heeded the yellow flags either. It was a tragic end for a talented driver.

The Siffert/Bell car won from Rodriguez/Oliver while Alfas took the next two spots from a Ferrari 512S. One of the Alfas was driven by Nanni Galli, Giunti's former regular co-driver and close friend. Galli admits today he never

Ignazio Giunti

Ignazio Giunti was from a wealthy family, and started racing in his teens. He raced mainly Alfa Romeos and was a works driver by 1966, doing much of the testing for the new Alfa Tipo 33 sports car. He was signed for Ferrari in 1970, doing four Grand Prix races and winning sports car events in the 512S. He was a very quick driver in everything he raced.

Ignazio Giunti as an Alfa driver in 1969. (Courtesy Ed McDonough)

Arturo Merzario

Arturo became well-known in the 1960s doing amazing things with sports and GT Abarths. His superb win at Mugello in 1969 got him an invitation to drive for Ferrari where he did many races in the 512S before becoming a regular in the 3-litre 312PB. He had a long Formula 1 career; running his own Merzario in 1978 and 1979. He remains active on the historic racing scene, mainly with Alfa Romeo for whom he also drove in sports cars in the mid-1970s.

Arturo Merzario and his familiar hat. (Courtesy Pete Austin)

really got over the loss of the man with whom he shared the bulk of the development work on the early Alfa T33s.

Daytona 24 Hours

The new Ferrari 512M had appeared in Buenos Aires in the hands of Mike Parkes and Jo Bonnier. It qualified eighth and finished seventh and, although a number of modifications had been incorporated, it still hadn't been sorted. However, when the cars all arrived in Florida for the Daytona 24 Hours on January 30-31, this car didn't appear, but there were 512M entries from NART and Roger Penske. The Penske Sunoco car for Mark Donohue and David Hobbs had been sorted and it looked like the Porsches might be facing a renewed Ferrari threat.

There were no works-entered Ferraris at Daytona. Ferrari hadn't intended to enter the new flat-12 car anyway, considering it undeveloped for a 24-hour event. There was a 312P, but it was chassis 0872, the coupé that had not very stylishly been converted to an open car, which was another NART entry for the interesting team of Luigi Chinetti Jr, Nestor Garcia Vega from Argentina, and the British driver Alain De Cadenet. Ferrari hadn't completed building a second 312P with the boxer engine, but that was now scheduled to replace 0874 in time for Sebring. However, the NART 312P didn't disgrace itself at all, though, sadly, all it had for company in Group 6 was a pair of Chevrons.

Donohue and Hobbs were on pole from Rodriguez/Oliver, Revson/Posey/Parsons in a 512M, Siffert/Bell, Gregory/Young, also in a 512M, and the 312P qualified 13th. Rodriguez and Oliver were told to act as the 'hare' to draw the Penske 512M into a hard sprint race, and that tactic worked ... sort of. Donohue led until Rodriguez went in front. Siffert and Bell were meant to hang back and eventually take over, but their engine went 'bang' after three and a half hours so that plan went out the window. Pedro just pushed on and extended his lead again, as Donohue started making stops to sort electrical problems and dropped to third. The 312P continued to make smooth progress and moved up the field. At midnight, the Elford 917 crashed in debris when one of the Corvettes hit the wall. Donohue slowed for the incident but he was then hit by a 911 which didn't slow down. The 512M lost 40 laps for repairs (this wouldn't be the only time that this car would run foul of Porsches!).

Rodriguez remained in front, from the NART 512S of

In the absence of any works Ferraris at Daytona, the North American Racing Team fielded 0872, now rebodied as an open car, for Chinetti Jr, Garcia Vega and De Cadenet. (Courtesy Lou Galanos)

Bucknam/Adamowicz and the little 312P. Donohue and Hobbs eventually managed, over the course of many hours, to fight their way back to third, as Pedro and Jackie Oliver won while the 312P was 5th behind one of the Corvettes in 4th, with Donohue 3rd.

Sebring 12 Hours

The Sebring race in 1971 marks the beginning of an odd relationship between the authors of this book and the new car which Ferrari delivered to the central Florida circuit. Ed McDonough was having his first and sadly only trip to the 12 Hours ... "one of the races I wished I had taken the trouble to go to more often." Peter Collins would start his association at the next race at Brands Hatch, where he photographed the car in its first European appearance.

Mario Andretti gets ready to practice in the first appearance of 0878 at Sebring. (Courtesy Ed McDonough)

Neither realised then that many years later they would be working together, testing this very same car and writing about it. So, this chapter becomes the story of a 312P as we follow it from the beginning of its career to the present day, a privilege for specialist journalists and an opportunity that doesn't come along that often.

Intensive work was done to get 0878 ready for Sebring. While the team was shocked at the death of Giunti in Argentina, the lessons were learned and the new car had an improved and strengthened monocoque structure. This and the improved headlights added weight to the car, but, nevertheless, it immediately looked a competitive package. It would be the only three-litre prototype that Ferrari would run for the bulk of the year, with a little surprise to come for the very end of the season. There have been stories that a further chassis had been built, or at least started, and that that had been cannibalized for 0878, but there's no firm evidence of this.

Andretti and Ickx were engaged to drive the new 312P, and a second NART car also arrived, this being the older 0872 with Chinetti Jr and George Eaton doing the driving. The JW Porsches were there, and there was one less 917 as one of the Martini cars had been badly damaged at Daytona, but Elford would share Dechent's second Martini car with Gerard Larrousse. Penske was back with a new 512M body for Donohue/Hobbs. Alfa Romeo had also skipped Daytona, and brought three cars which looked very quick in testing.

Donohue arrived at the circuit late for practice, as he'd an injured ankle and had been driving the Penske transporter when it broke down. Practice had been very relaxed, quite warm with no rain, and everyone was concentrating on reliability for the hard airfield circuit which makes great demands on brakes and gearboxes, and rewards lightness, good handling and reasonable power. However, when Donohue got himself focussed, he put the blue and yellow 512M on pole, though Mario Andretti had 0878 just behind him in second. Rodriguez and Oliver were third, Elford/Larrousse 4th, and the Alfa of Galli/Stommeln 5th.

At the start Donohue blasted away from everyone, and really wanted to stay out of everybody's path in this race. The three 917s, Andretti and the Revson 512M

Jacky Ickx accelerates out of the Sebring Hairpin. (Courtesy Ed McDonough)

fought amongst themselves as the Penske car went away. Co-author McDonough went off to see as much of the circuit as possible and in the first hour witnessed Donohue and Siffert sit about four seconds apart as Rodriguez and Andretti followed behind. While the 512M and the 917s had a speed advantage on the long straight sections, Andretti was braking later and nipping through the medium and slow corners much quicker, keeping in touch with the bigger cars. Elford went off course and was forced to pit and Revson was also delayed. When Donohue pitted, Siffert led but over-extended himself and ran out of fuel. He was penalised four minutes for accepting a ride back to the pits.

As Ed McDonough worked his way round the circuit he watched Gregg Young in the 512M shared with Masten Gregory have its throttle stick open exiting a hairpin. It went up the embankment and rolled on its side and burst into flames, though Young got out.

Andretti had built up a good lead which Jacky Ickx extended as they had much better fuel consumption. After some four hours, the 312P was leading comfortably. Donohue and Rodriguez were having a close fight for second place as they approached the chicane at the start of the back straight. A slower car moved into Donohue's line and he moved over to go by, and Pedro did more or less the same thing. Donohue would claim that Pedro moved too

NART's spider-bodied 0872 appeared again for Chinetti Jr and George Eaton. (Courtesy Ed McDonough)

quickly and the two cars collided damaging the right front of the 917 and the left side of the 512M. Ed McDonough was just approaching this spot when it occurred and hurried back to the pits to see what was going on:

"Both cars were being repaired. Donohue was furious and he was accusing Pedro, John Wyer was having a go at Penske, Porsche people argued with Ferrari people. I slid up to Pedro and asked what happened. 'He reversed into me' he said quietly, with one of his great disarming smiles."

Then at the halfway point disaster struck 0878. The gearbox stopped working and Ickx was stuck out on the circuit. The Elford/Larrousse Martini 917 had worked back up to 2nd so took the lead but immediately pitted. The Alfa T33/3 of Galli/Stommeln was suddenly leading a major endurance race. In the final hours the 917 moved back up front, but two Alfas were in contention and, when the Rodriguez 917 needed more bodywork, Elford/Larrousse just took the win from Galli/Stommeln and the second Alfa of de Adamich/Pescarolo/Vaccarella, with Rodriguez/Oliver

Andretti on the pit straight in 0878. (Courtesy Ed McDonough)

4th, Siffert/Bell 5th, and Donohue/Hobbs a very annoyed 6th. The NART 312P chassis 0872 again trundled home, this time 8th.

This had been Ed McDonough's first trip to Sebring – a chance to see a straight battle between the 512 and 917 on a wide-open circuit. He was also fortunate enough to have time to examine 0878 and talk to Jacky Ickx, who said the 312P was very much like the Grand Prix car. It gave a shock to the Porsche 917s with its excellent handling and could get round the bigger cars in the corners. Although the gearbox broke after 117 laps, the car was very competitive. Despite having twin fuel tanks, all the fuel was carried in the left tank to balance the driver's weight. It had been designed with this in mind, and this car still runs in this format.

Brands Hatch 1000 Kilometres

The Championship contenders headed to Brands Hatch for the first European race of the year on April 4. As practice developed for the 1000 Kilometres, it became clear that the former Group 4 cars, now Group 5, 5-litre sports cars, would soon be eclipsed by the newer three-litre prototypes.

Clay Regazzoni was Jacky Ickx's partner in 0878 for this race, and again the Ferrari factory sent only the one car. There were several Porsche 917s as usual, but only the JW cars seemed to be on the pace, and also a handful of Ferrari 512Ms, with the car of Herbert Muller and Rene Herzog looking to have potential. This was one of the cars that had started life as a 512S before being converted to 512M specs. Autodelta brought its continually improved 3-litre Tipo 33/3s, and they were lighter, and quicker. For the first time 2-litre Group 6 cars were making a serious impression, as both the Lola 212 and the Chevron B19 and B16 were qualifying well up the grid, ahead of some of the 917s. There were also some British-built machines of interest – the Huron, the Martin and the Dulon-Porsche. This latter car would gain a degree of notoriety.

0878 had been further lightened for Brands Hatch, with the Sebring lighting arrangement now removed and some improvements to the bodywork. Regazzoni was quick to get to grips with the car and began putting in very impressive times. He and Ickx put the 'smaller' Ferrari firmly on pole, and a sign of the changing times was the first of the Alfa T33s next to him, Stommeln and Hezemans having also gone very well. This meant the JW Porsches of Siffert/Bell and Rodriguez/Oliver were 3rd and 4th, with the Elford/Redman 917 5th and Pescarolo and de Adamich 6th in another Alfa.

Jacky Ickx

Ickx, along with Clay Regazzoni, drove in more races in the 312P period than any of the other top-line drivers in the Ferrari team. His Grand Prix career spanned 14 seasons, giving him a number of wins but the World Championship eluded him. He was active in motor cycle racing before moving to cars, taking part in virtually every category of competition. He became a master of Le Mans, won the CanAm title and drove sports cars for all the major teams. He was a member of both the Ferrari F1 and sports car teams at a time when a good development driver was essential, and he contributed much to the Scuderia's success. Ickx is still a leading figure in motor racing, holding a number of important administrative posts.

Jacky Ickx.
(Courtesy Peter Collins)

Jacky Ickx in 0878 in its first European appearance in practice at Brands Hatch. (Courtesy Pete Austin)

0878 attracts a crowd in the Brands Hatch paddock during practice. (Courtesy Peter Collins)

Co-author Peter Collins captured Regazzoni in Druids Bend during practice. (Courtesy Peter Collins)

It rained before the start and the Kent track was quite wet as the flag came down. Ickx took 0878 away from the pack immediately to give himself a comfortable lead, and it began to look like 1970 all over again as Rodriguez got the jump on the Alfa and teammate Siffert and was up into second. Siffert was next as the other 917s slid around on the wet track, and John Miles pulled the Chevron B19 all the way up to 6th from the back.

Rodriguez caught Ickx in 0878 and the two cars tore around the Brands circuit in close formation. They were lapping the slower cars and Ickx came upon Bill Mc Govern driving Martin Ridehalgh's Dulon-Porsche which was having its second spin. This time, it forced Ickx off the track and into the banking. Ickx managed to get the car out but it bore the scars of contact on the side and the front was seriously damaged. He came into the pits and 0878 lost

The start of the 1000 Kilometres, with Ickx on the inside, an Alfa T33 alongside, and a horde of five-litre cars right behind. (Courtesy Peter Collins)

Jacky Ickx set the early pace as the track dried after the damp start. (Courtesy Peter Collins)

Ickx shows the ability of the 312P to hold off the JW 917 Porsche. (Courtesy Peter Collins)

When Regazzoni was behind the wheel, he showed that he, too, could fend off the 917. (Courtesy Peter Collins)

eight laps being repaired. This allowed the JW cars to lead, now with two Alfas behind them.

Ickx dropped to the back of the field but was absolutely flying, getting himself back into the top ten before handing over. Regazzoni then moved up another five places. Then Rodriguez retired, and at the halfway stage, Siffert/Bell were overtaken when they had to refuel earlier than the Group 6 Alfas, which went into a somewhat surprising lead. Siffert was coming back but Bell later had a stop to change a wheel and the nut jammed on, damaging the thread. As the race went on, the two Alfas cruised around in the lead for an hour, Stommeln/Hezemans in front. Then the engine packed up when Hezemans was driving. Ickx was back in the Ferrari and flying again, though the car was having problems at the pit stops with a jammed starter motor. That prevented them from catching the Pescarolo/de Adamich T33 which took a long overdue win.

The Siffert/Bell 917 managed to get back up to 3rd, ahead of the Herzog/Muller 512M. It had been a superb race.

Regazzoni pushes 0878 hard through Westfield Bend. (Courtesy Peter Collins)

Though disappointed over not winning, Regazzoni was enthusiastic about the car in this Italian radio interview. (Courtesy Peter Collins)

51

Clay Regazzoni

The Swiss driver began his career in the 1960s in F3 and F2 Brabhams before moving to Tecno, where he became a works driver. He had a reputation as a very tough and forceful driver, something that earned him a number of critics. He was a Ferrari F1 pilot from 1970 through 1972, and after a year with BRM, returned to the Ferrari fold for three more seasons. Like some of his peers, he drove sports cars for both Ferrari and Alfa Romeo. He was more successful in sports cars, though he had a number of wins throughout his long GP career, which ended with a major crash at Long Beach in the Ensign in 1980. This left him paralyzed but undaunted, he had Ferrari GTs converted to hand controls so he could still compete in events. He loved historic rallies and was very competent, and was a good friend to the authors, always willing to share his experiences. At a retro Targa Florio he sat bemused after dinner as the Italian event organizers tried to set fastest laps around the hotel lobby in his wheelchair!

Clay Regazzoni. (Courtesy Pete Austin)

Monza 1000 Kilometres

Three weeks after Brands Hatch, Monza was the scene of what was expected to be a very high-speed duel between the 5-litre cars. This happened to take place in the race rather more than in qualifying, as it happened. Ickx and Regazzoni were back with 0878 which had body repairs after its Dulon incident in the UK. There were six Porsche 917s and several Ferrari 512Ms. Elford was quickest in the Martini 917 but these cars didn't look quite so much like winners as the JW cars. Ickx and Regazzoni were next up, proving that even at Monza the 3-litre Group 6 cars were able to match the bigger machines. The rest of the Porsches and the Alfa Romeos were next, with the odd Ferrari getting near the front.

In the race, the JW cars just sprinted away from everyone, and Rodriguez and Siffert were to set incredible lap times around Monza. The 312P was not far off the pace but, on its 11th lap, Merzario in the 512M made contact with another car and three machines were damaged and out. One of them was 0878. The JW 917s ran away with the win but all three Alfa Tipo 33s finished well, and were

Ickx in 0878 in the wet at Monza, passing a Chevron B-19. (Courtesy Archiv Fodisch)

increasingly reliable. Again, 0878 looked to have winning potential, and no-one would have guessed that it would have only one more decent placing.

Spa 1000 Kilometres

The Group 6 entry for Spa, only two weeks after Monza, was small, consisting of the 312P, a single Alfa Tipo 33 for Pescarolo and de Adamich, a 908 for Ballot Lena and Chasseuil, and two 2-litre cars. These were the former Chevron now known as the Redex Special for Tony Goodwin, and the 'infamous' Dulon-Porsche. There was a 2-litre car in Group 5, the Chevron B8 of Tony Birchenough and Brian Joscelyne.

Ickx and Regazzoni were back in 0878 which had had a thorough rebuild after its involvement in the Monza accident, its second crash in two races. The JW Porsche 917s which had run with long tails at Monza were back to the short rear for Spa, mainly because the bumpy surface threw the car around. The Martini team, however, opted for the long-tail. Siffert and Bell were on pole, Bell revelling in the speed of the 'old circuit', while Elford and Larrousse were next, with Rodriguez/Oliver 3rd. Marko and van Lennep in the other Martini 917 were 4th, and Ickx and Regazzoni were 5th, six seconds off pole time, but only two seconds slower than the Martini 917.

Though there was a brief localized shower before the start, the JW cars stayed on dry tyres ... and disappeared. During the first hour, the two leaders kept breaking the lap record, leaving it at over 162mph. With the Martini cars and the 512Ms not doing anything special, Ickx and Regazzoni held third in 0878. The de Adamich Alfa was 4th but dropped back as the bodywork started to come apart.

Clay Regazzoni was usually very quick at Spa. (Courtesy Brian Joscelyne)

As the JW 917s pulled away by several laps, 0878 held 3rd for much of the race. Then fate intervened as the Ferrari came up to pass the Dulon-Porsche of Martin Ridehalgh and Ian Taylor. The two cars collided exactly as they had at Brands Hatch and headed for the pits. The Dulon was out after 40 laps, and the Ferrari managed 51. Though it was 8th on the road, it wasn't running at the finish and was thus unclassified.

The JW cars won by four laps, had a new record, and the Pescarolo/de Adamich Alfa was a good third. Not a single Ferrari was classified, as one of the private 917s managed 4th.

Ferrari claimed industrial strife prevented it from sending any works cars to the Targa Florio, and, in fact, there was not a single 512. Porsche was there in strength but the weekend belonged to Alfa Romeo. The great local hero Nino Vaccarella set fastest qualifying lap and, with Toine Hezemans, won the event from teammates de Adamich and van Lennep. Porsche didn't get a look in.

Nürburgring 1000 Kilometres

Then it was immediately to Germany for the Nürburgring 1000 Kilometres on May 20. It was clear that the Group 6 cars would be at an advantage on the swoops and dives of the 'Ring, and only the private Jost/Kauhsen 917 was there, all the other competitive Porsche entries being 908/3s for both the JW and Martini teams. Alfas were there in strength and again looking good after the Targa win.

Jacky Ickx showed just how good yet another rebuild had been for 0878 when he put it on pole by an amazing nine seconds from the next quickest car, the T33 of Galli/Stommeln. The Martini cars of Elford/Larrousse and van Lennep/Marko were next from Bell/Siffert, with Rodriguez sharing that car with Bell and Siffert as well, though it was originally intended for Oliver. The other Alfas were next in line.

There was a Ferrari 512M and a 512S, and the Dulon-Porsche was there again, making Ickx and Regazzoni nervous. Ickx pulled out a five second lead on the first lap and extended it to over 40 seconds by five laps. Second was being fought out by Stommeln's Alfa and the 908/3s of Elford, Siffert and Rodriguez, with de Adamich's T33 next. Then on the sixth lap Ickx came flying in to say the car was overheating, so water was added to the radiator. This dropped him to fourth as the lead trio went past, but Siffert was in the next time round with the Porsche's under tray coming loose. This left an Alfa Romeo in the lead and Ickx was running cautiously in 6th. As the other cars came in for scheduled stops at quarter distance, Ickx moved up to third, and yet again the Ferrari's chances of a win looked good as two laps later Ickx was in front. When the Galli/Stommeln Alfa dropped out Ickx had a very sizable lead, and Regazzoni took over without losing it.

Then the halfway mark was signalled by a trail of blue haze from the Ferrari. When Regazzoni came in, the radiator was refilled but it poured straight out of the exhausts. That was it again for 0878. The Martini 908/3 of Elford/Larrousse won from Rodriguez/Siffert despite the brave attempts of Helmut Marko to get past Rodriguez in the final stages. The two surviving Alfas were 4th and 5th ahead of the private 917. Porsches took 16 of the first 20 places.

Hans Dieter Dechent's Martini team rubbed in the 'Ring victory at Le Mans three weeks later when the Marko/van Lennep 917 won from the Attwood/Muller JW car and two Ferrari 512Ms. The first prototype home was a 2-litre Porsche 907. Ferrari and Alfa Romeo had decided not to run at the 24-hour races at Daytona and Le Mans, so there was no Le Mans appearance for 0878 or any of the T33s.

American photographer Fred Lewis caught this dramatic shot of Ickx in 0878 at the Nürburgring. (Courtesy Fred Lewis)

Österreichring 1000 Kilometres

June 27 was the date of the Österreichring 1000 Kilometres, with Ferrari, Alfa Romeo and JW Porsche all trying to get one over on the Martini Porsches. Regazzoni and Ickx were back after the break from Le Mans and they put 0878 on the front row of the grid, but they were a few tenths off the pace of the 917 driven by Pedro Rodriguez and Richard Attwood. Jackie Oliver had left for CanAm so Attwood took over. Pedro was at the top of his form, incredibly fast in the Porsche 917, and he'd been winning for BRM. The Marko/Larrousse Martini car was next from Siffert/Bell and the 512M of Muller/Herzog.

Rodriguez led the first half dozen away from the pack very quickly, with 0878 on his tail. They caught the backmarkers in a few laps. When Juncadella moved the Spanish Ferrari 512M off-line to let them past he lost it

0878's serious run of bad fortune continued at the Österreichring where it was damaged in a crash.

and rolled several times, though he was fine. After the first round of stops, Ickx was 45 seconds in front, and Rodriguez had pitted early for electrical problems to be sorted. Siffert retired the JW 917 with a broken clutch, and Regazzoni took over and led. Then Marko got by him briefly, but the Swiss driver was soon back in front. Rodriguez was flying and moved up the field when it started to rain. When Ickx went back into 0878, he was still first, with Larrousse/Marko and Rodriguez/Attwood both on the same lap as the Ferrari.

Attwood took over from Pedro for the minimal period. When they swapped places, Pedro was a lap down on Marko, but then the Martini car hit the barriers and was out. On lap 132, Regazzoni again replaced Ickx and Rodriguez came in for fuel. The Mexican was over a lap down on the 312P, but in ten laps had unlapped himself and roared away to try and make up the deficit. On lap 149 Regazzoni lost the Ferrari under braking, aided by a suspension problem. The Ferrari was quite severely crumpled and yet another sure win was lost. Ing.Caliri said the car had just given up and that's why it crashed.

Rodriguez finished one of his very best drives, and won from two Alfas and a private 512M. The 312P was 5th on the track but wasn't running at the finish and was unclassified.

Two weeks later, Rodriguez was killed at the Norisring Interseries race in one of Herbert Muller's Ferrari 512Ms. Fans realised they had seen his last great performance in Austria.

Watkins Glen 6-Hour Race

The weekend of the Watkins Glen 6-Hour Race was almost always a celebration in the beautiful mountain country of upper New York State. Not only was there the build-up to the Six Hours and the race itself, but there also a CanAm race on the day after the sports cars had their fling, which meant that several of the sports cars could have a straight fight with the CanAm big-bangers.

It also meant that co-author McDonough could renew his acquaintance with 0878 which he had seen in March at Sebring. The same pairing of Ickx and Andretti was in the car which had been rebuilt yet again ... there must be a record there! There was a feeling of sadness at the Glen as Pedro Rodriguez – a great favourite there – was now gone, replaced in the JW squad by Gijs van Lennep.

This was to be the last Championship race for the 5-litre Group 5 cars, and there were hopes that a Ferrari might beat the Porsches. Mark Donohue and David Hobbs were out again in Roger Penske's Sunoco 512M, and set the quickest time in qualifying, with Siffert/van Lennep next: again, the 312P was well up there in 3rd. only a tiny bit slower. The Bell/Attwood JW 917 was 4th.

Donohue moved immediately into a good lead and the two JW 917s were in a Ferrari sandwich as Ickx was right on their tails and went past them within the first half hour of the race. Siffert was then slowed by a puncture, Bell had the throttle break and they both dropped down the order. After

The Belgian driver was on exactly the same line, lap after lap. (Courtesy Ed McDonough)

Mario Andretti made a few adjustments before his serious qualifying run. (Courtesy Ed McDonough)

The cars gather on the grid for the start. Again, 0878 is ahead of the bigger 5-litre Ferraris. (Courtesy Ed McDonough)

The JW Porsches gave Ickx a hard time at Watkins Glen. (Courtesy Ed McDonough)

one hour, Donohue suddenly had the suspension collapse and Ickx powered into the lead ... again! At his pit stop, however, the starter motor wouldn't work and Andretti was deprived of a drive. 0878 was retired ... again! The Alfa T33 of de Adamich and Ronnie Peterson had been going well and inherited the lead. The two JW 917s couldn't catch up so the Alfa won with the team car of Galli/Elford not making the finish while in 4th. Peterson was having a try-out in the Alfa as a possible driver for 1972 ... he was a bit surprised at the win.

Imola 500 Kilometres

With a long break until the next race, Ferrari was now concentrating on F1, of course, but was also working very hard to construct the new sports car for 1972, the 312PB. In the meantime, 0878 would get another work-out back on Ferrari home territory ... Imola.

It was not entirely clear why Ferrari would have decided to send a car to an Interseries race meeting, aside from the possibility of securing reasonable start and prize money. Though this was called the Imola 500 Kilometres, it was, in fact, a race in two heats and a final, and Group 5 and 6 cars were admitted to bolster the small number of unlimited Group 7 machines. The first heat would be for cars up to 3-litres and the second for the others, with so many of each plus the fastest twelve into the final.

0878 was entered for Regazzoni and this would guarantee a large Italian crowd. Peter Schetty was testing the car on Thursday but seemed to be taking it pretty easy. The Ferrari would be up against some quick Alfa T33s as well as the bigger machinery. On Friday, in official qualifying, Regazzoni put his foot down and soon broke the outright circuit record. Zeccoli was out in the Alfa 33TT3 tubular chassis car which had appeared several times but only in practice. He managed to bend it in an attempt to hang onto 0878, so it again didn't race.

Enzo Ferrari was present on Saturday to see if Regazzoni could win a special trophy for the first car to break the 200kph lap speed. Even with Commendatore standing at the pit wall, Regazzoni was just failing to average 200kph by a few hundredths of a second. Peter Gethin was second quickest in the big McLaren M8E and Jo Bonnier had his 8.1-litre Lola T222 in third. There was a final session with the trophy and cash prizes for fastest in each class and that meant there was some very hard driving indeed. Regazzoni finally made Ferrari happy with his time, but then Gethin went a shade quicker. Brian Redman was also quick in the BRM P154.

Heat One on Sunday started in the wet and continued in the wet. Regazzoni shot away and led the first lap from Merzario in a 2-litre Abarth by 13 seconds. As the rain came down harder Regazzoni gave a great wet weather driving exhibition. Facetti in an Alfa caught Merzario. On lap 23 the Austrian Klaus Reisch in a private T33/3 spun on the pit straight and hit the wall, Reisch being thrown out and the car bursting into flames. Reisch died from his injuries and the race ran out under a cloud in more ways than one.

That looked like it would turn out to be the only victory by 0878 in its long and hard career, and though it was only a heat win, it showed how much promise the car always had. In Heat 2, Redman's BRM beat Leo Kinnunen in the Porsche 917 Spyder in even wetter conditions. The Final was then reduced to only ten laps instead of thirty, but Clay Regazzoni looked like he might beat the giants in a straight fight, especially as it was wet, though the rain had stopped. Regazzoni outran Redman and the big BRM into the first corner, but by Tosa the Ferrari fuel pump had stuck, not for the first time, and Regga pulled over and retired as Redman won the Final, and the event overall on aggregate from Facetti's Alfa and Merzario.

0878 had put in a lot of racing in 1971 and had been in several accidents, so Scuderia Ferrari decided it needed a complete rebuild ... again! Much of the original car remained, though it incorporated features that would appear in the 1972 cars. This is one reason it is sometimes referred to as a PB, but always in retrospect. It also was re-numbered 0880. The changes were not dramatic. They included lower profile tires, which gave a wider track and a slight bulge in the rear body section. The height was slightly reduced, and, as the weight limits had been changed, additional strengthening was built into the chassis, and the size of some of the chassis tubing was increased slightly; but in spite of this, the car was not very different.

Kyalami Nine Hour Race

In November 1971, the revised 0880/0878 was sent to Kyalami in South Africa for the Nine-Hour Race, a non-championship but important event. The first of the 1972 PBs – 0882 – was also sent. At the time, 0882 was announced as the first of the seven 1972 PBs (0882, 0884, 0886, 0888, 0890, 0892, 0894) and this strengthens the argument that Ferrari saw all the previous cars as 312Ps. We will deal in detail with the new 312PB in the next chapter.

Brian Redman, after a time with JW and a good drive at Imola in the Interseries BRM, was signed to drive for Ferrari. He was to partner Regazzoni in 0880/0878, the car which had seen so much service throughout the year. Ickx and Mario Andretti would be in the new car, and it was the new car which began to make the pace in the first practice sessions. The opposition was coming from two David Piper Porsche 917s for Attwood/Charlton and Mario Casoni/Tony Adamowicz. Then there was a horde of 2-litre Chevron B-19s, and some Lola T212s, and then a real mixed bag filled the rest of the grid.

Redman made Ferrari sit up and take notice when he started to drive the 'old car' very quickly. He made some changes to the rear roll bars and dampers, and then set pole time under Dave Charlton's F1 lap record. The other team car was next, and also on the front row was the B-19 Chevron-Vega of Hailwood and Craft.

At the start, Regazzoni quickly moved into the lead. Andretti had a misfire on the first lap and lost several places. In thirty minutes Regazzoni had lapped the field, with Adamowicz and Attwood behind him. At one hour, with Andretti having worked the other Ferrari back up to second, a familiar scenario was unfolding. The 1971 312P seemed to have it in the bag. Then the inevitable occurred. Adamowicz was spun by a backmarker just as Regazzoni was coming by, and the two cars hit each other and headed for the pits. How many times had we seen that this year?

Redman replaced his teammate and a new front body section was fitted. Andretti was leading but soon stopped out on the circuit, seemingly out of fuel. That car lost 45 minutes before it was back in the pits and running again. Thus, the Hailwood/Craft Chevron was leading, but soon after they lost their engine. Redman and Regazzoni were then given a two-lap penalty for having five mechanics work on the car. However, this didn't stop Redman from getting into and extending his lead. 0880/0878 was having

Brian Redman

Redman enjoyed success from the beginning of his varied career, doing well in F2, and winning in Lolas and Porsches. He rather 'played' with F1 between 1968 and 1974, but was a very serious sports car driver for Lola, Porsche and Ferrari, as well as being a front runner in CanAm. After retiring from professional racing, he remained involved as an organiser and still competes in historic events around the world.

Brain Redman made his Ferrari debut at Kyalami. (Courtesy Pete Austin)

one of its best races, though, of course, it always did that and then stopped. By half distance Redman led John Hine, and then Hailwood in the Gunston team's other car. Ickx and Andretti had moved back up to second. Over the next few hours Redman and Regazzoni dominated at the front, other cars had problems, and Ickx and Andretti were really moving up the field.

The new Ferrari made it back up into second place, but Regazzoni was now 15 laps in front, an incredible job for him and Redman in the 'old car'. Ferrari was ecstatic over the result and that really gave it an incentive for the coming year. Meanwhile, Paddy Driver, Mike Hailwood and Howden Ganley were third in the Chevron B-19-FVC, with Adamowicz/Casoni 4th, and Helmut Marko and John Love 5th in a Lola T212 FVC.

Porsche won the 1971 Manufacturers' Championship with 85 points to 54 for Alfa Romeo and 26 for Ferrari. Porsche also took the Grand Touring Trophy, the Challenge Mondiale and Triple Crown points. Had there been a proper sports car driver's championship that year, it would have gone to Porsche's Pedro Rodriguez by nine points from Alfa Romeo's Andrea de Adamich, and Jo Siffert another eleven points behind.

When the 1972 Le Mans test days came in April, 0880/0878 reappeared for some of the practice sessions, and then was not seen again until the Targa Florio where it was used as a practice car for Merzario and rally driver Sandro Munari. The practice must have helped because Merzario/Munari won the great Sicilian race, but in chassis 0884. That was then the end of the car's rather astonishing period career, in which it had done not only a large number of races, but test sessions, practices and development work as well.

The continuing history of 0880/0878

Not only did 0878 reappear as 0880, it also made an appearance in 1972, as we'll learn, but then disappeared for a very long time.

The car spent time in the collections of Albert Obrist and Bernie Ecclestone, and of the Japanese collector Yoshijuki Hayashi. It was in the hands of Michael Vernon in the UK, and then appeared at the Cavallino Classic event at Moroso with Scott Code. American Bill Binnie found it in 2000 and had it restored by Paul Lanzante in the south of England, though it was already in pretty good condition, suffering mainly from neglect and lack of use or attention. Enzo Ferrari believed that a private team could never run one of these cars, but, of course, he was proved wrong.

Paul Lanzante's team brought the car to a test track for a full day to give the opportunity of stripping the bodywork and examining it in detail, as well as to provide the chance for a serious driving test. The authors were finally able to look closely at the steel tube/aluminum centre tub to which is attached the engine, transmission, steering, suspension and brakes from the 1971 312B F1 car. The flat-12 engine has a short stroke, 78.5mm bore and 51.5mm stroke, allowing it to rev easily to 11,000rpm, at which point it produces 440bhp – a bit less than the F1 car with about 150kg more weight to carry. The car was on Avon tires at the time of our test, intermediates, 13 x 25 x 15 at the rear and 9 x 20 x 13 at the front. One needs to remember that these low profile tires were considered revolutionary when they first appeared, and that they changed the shape of prototypes significantly and for all time. In combination with the new wedge-shape, the aerodynamics also changed, as did wing location and size, and the use of aerodynamic trim fences became an art form. What Richie Ginther had started at Ferrari in 1960 with rough little pieces of metal as tiny spoilers had advanced enormously in 11-12 years. By 1971, much more attention was being paid to air-flow through and around openings and radiators, and this car, particularly, was often, though not always, seen with two small upright stabilizers at the rear in front of the adjustable rear tab.

The car in the form we tested it showed all of its old promise with good results in an historic race at Spa, and was running well at Rockingham at the historic festival before a spin onto the then unfinished infield did a lot of damage to the floorpan, puncturing it in several places and creating the dilemma of how to repair it without changing its

The 1971 312P chassis 0878 about to be tested by the authors. (Courtesy Peter Collins)

character. Bill Binnie allowed Ed McDonough to drive the car because it needed some track time with newly installed and modern data logging computer equipment. The idea was to run several steady but not slow laps to get the new equipment working, and then test it a bit further.

Usually, a track test allows the driver to build up familiarity with the car and investigate its characteristics as you drive. This time, however, we were running in new equipment so it was important to get down to the job from the beginning. The data logging equipment took up most of the floor of the 'passenger' side of the car – yes, the 312P has a passenger seat, of a kind, a red and black period seat like the driver's. The Momo Ferrari steering wheel is very much F1, as is the general fit and feel of the seat which gives lots of lateral support, as it would have to hour after hour in endurance races. Jacky Ickx and Derek Bell both told me that the 312P was like driving an F1 car in comfort!

In the seat, you are aware of the fuel tanks on either side, though only the left one is used as was mentioned earlier to balance the driver's weight. The instruments are period F1, with a large rev counter in the dominant position and a temperature/pressure gauge incorporating almost all the other functions. And there's a horn! This is left over from that Targa Florio practice session in 1972 and is a very

Uncovering the front end of 0878. (Courtesy Peter Collins)

important reminder of this car's history. The tall mirror in the centre works well, though the side mirrors vibrate and cover only the blind spot on each side, so at least you know if someone's there.

The gear change sits to the right, with the sliding metal bars located under the gate in true Ferrari fashion to prevent going down more than one gear at a time and making the revs jump too far. It turns out to be a beautiful gearbox and is wonderful to use. The modern computer equipment allows very good feedback to the crew on braking, throttle and steering positions, rpm, and basically tells the team in the pit what mistakes you're making. It definitely makes the driver more honest!

Then it comes time to drive the car. Ed McDonough very much regrets that he went to Sebring only once, that time back in 1971. He didn't think then a time would come in the future when he wished he had gone to many, many more races, talked to more drivers and taken more photos. Fortunately, he had picked a good year to go. Mark Donohue and David Hobbs were really giving the Porsche

The Ferrari flat-12 engine, the same unit as in the Grand Prix car. (Courtesy Peter Collins)

The Ferrari 5-speed gear change. (Courtesy Peter Collins)

The Ferrari's Momo steering wheel. (Courtesy Peter Collins)

The shapely and purposeful lines of the flat-12 312P. (Courtesy Peter Collins)

917s a hard time with the Penske Sunoco Ferrari 512M. They dominated practice and looked set for a fine performance.

Alongside Donohue on the grid was 'our' car, chassis 0878, on the front row after Ickx and Andretti had pushed it very hard in the Florida sun to put Pedro Rodriguez and the other 917s a further row back. Andretti and Ickx were in relaxed form all weekend. Ickx was exceptionally talkative for that period in his career when he was known as not the easiest person to talk to, and Andretti was as easy-going as ever. They looked like they could win this race, but the gearbox, which was now being tested by us, had other ideas. Vic Elford, in fact, was the winner in the 917 in Martini colours.

So, that was the long story leading up to the co-author being behind the wheel of this historic machine:

"However, 30 years earlier the driver didn't have to share the car with a computer which told everyone the mistakes you made. This made my drive very focussed and smooth, not wanting to record any errors. The car helped because, by its nature, it's very smooth. The engine has fantastic but manageable torque combined with such a superb gearbox. The acceleration is almost blinding, but easy to control, and the engine propels the light car out of corners with the most sensational noise – a sort of 'waaaaang' – and it gathers momentum so rapidly. It was at the braking point so quickly

Ed McDonough experiences the acceleration of the flat-12 engine. (Courtesy Peter Collins)

that I had to force myself to be smooth and systematic, not wanting to send messages back on the computer that I was jumping on the brakes. The steering was neutral and in the corners the grip can be found early and used, with neither understeer nor oversteer. The steering provides lots of feel so you know what is happening all the time. At higher speeds the firmness and stiff suspension means you have to pay attention when accelerating hard, but this seemed to come quickly. Even with a reasonable rev limit, the car was going very quickly, and in top gear was reaching 150mph with no difficulty at all, with that additional 30mph easily available!

"0878/0880 was amazing for the lack of drama. It was very precise, and it was always possible to know what the

0878 displayed slight roll in medium speed corners, but was very sure-footed. (Courtesy Peter Collins)

back end was doing. Once the gear change was mastered, I was back there at Sebring, out on the long stretches of bumpy airfield runway looking out for Ferrari 512s and Porsche 917s, ready to turn into the Esses and whip past under braking, or come past the Martini 917 at the Hairpin on the outside, watching Vic Elford blink as he realized what happened. I saw that happen and now I was doing it!"

Brian Redman talks about 0880/0878

After our experience of being able to examine and drive 0880/0878, we caught up with Brian Redman; after all, he'd had a pretty good time with it, too!

"I was at the non-championship sports car race at Imola in 1971, driving the BRM CanAm car. The Tony Southgate-designed cars were very good in the wet and it rained through the whole race. I lapped the field and won the race. Ferrari was there and after the race Mauro Forghieri came up to me and asked what I was doing in 1972, and asked me then and there if I would like to join Ferrari. Ferrari had

67

been running the 312P all through 1971 and had been competitive, but up to that point I don't think they had won a race. So we took two cars to Kyalami for the Nine-Hour Race in November. Clay Regazzoni and I ran the old car, while Mario Andretti and Jacky Ickx had a new one. Regazzoni and I had a great weekend, qualifying on pole position and then leading the entire race to win. Ickx and Andretti had some problems and they finished second.

"There were differences between the sports car and the F1 car. Whenever you get a lighter car, running on wide tires, you get essentially better handling. Though the 917s weighed about 1800 pounds, the Ferrari was lighter; I would say about 1300-1400 pounds. Now in 1970-71, when there was no minimum weight, the Porsche 908-3, based on the Bergspyder, weighed only 1100 pounds, and it was tremendously quick, but it only had 370bhp. So Porsche argued very hard that the same rules be applied for 1972; that is, no minimum weight. But the FIA said no and that is why the 312PB became heavier but also stronger. The 908 was about as quick around the Nürburgring as the 312P and PB. So the 312P was in many ways like the F1 car, just heavier. The only problem was that it wasn't quite strong enough for 24 hours, so that's why Ferrari didn't do Le Mans in 1972. Basically, the 312P had an F1 engine with slightly different camshafts and lower revs. That's why it was so good to drive."

Specifications 1971 312P

Chassis	Space-frame with riveted aluminum panels
Bodywork	Fibreglass
Front track	1425mm
Rear track	1400mm
Wheelbase	2220mm
Weight	650kg
Suspension	Front: independent with unequal length upper and lower wishbones and coil-over springs. Rear: independent with lower wishbone and upper links and coil-over springs
Engine type	Flat-12, twin overhead camshafts, 4 valves per cylinder, electronic ignition
Bore & stroke	78.5mm x 51.5mm
Capacity	2991cc
Horsepower	450bhp @ 10,500rpm
Fuel delivery	Lucas fuel injection
Gearbox	5-speed and reverse
Brakes	Outboard discs front and rear
Wheels	13 x 10 front; 15 x 15.5 rear

Visit Veloce on the web – www.veloce.co.uk
Details of all books in print • Special offers • New book news • Gift vouchers • Web forum • And much more ...

1972 – Ferrari 312PB flat-12 – Packing a punch

It had taken motorsport's governing body, the CSI, two years to catch up with the fabulously entertaining sports car racing rules and enforce its own idea of the future on the World Sportscar Championship. No more were the wonderfully ferocious Ferrari 512s and Porsche 917s to be allowed to provide great entertainment for the spectators. In the interests of cost and safety – those catch-all reasons for most killjoy rule-making – from January 1st 1972, there was to be an overall international sports car racing capacity limit of 3 litres.

As we have seen, Enzo Ferrari saw this coming and had dropped the 512 project like a hot potato for 1971 in favour of his little 312P '180-degree 12-cylinder' car. In *Motor Sport* magazine Denis Jenkinson had said: "If ever a Grand Prix car was thinly disguised to run as a sports car it is the Ferrari 312P, for if you remove the fibreglass bodyshell you have a 312B (that year's Ferrari GP machine), and it is a splendid machine." He went on: "Armed with the flat-12 cylindered, 3-litre, thinly-disguised GP cars, the Ferrari team are going to set a pretty hot pace in 1972."

It was not entirely true that the 312P was a 312B with a two-seater body, as it had a wider and strengthened chassis, but it was as close as makes no difference. While mentioning this, perhaps we should repeat the fact that 'B' and 'P,' the titles of all these cars, are often misquoted. So, to clear things up, the 1969 sports prototypes were 312P, the 1971 cars were also 312P, but with the added rider that they were '180-degree V-12' cars, which we refer to consistently as flat-12. The upcoming 1972 cars were logically given the title of 312PB as they were the 'B,' second, or Mark 2 version of the 1971 312P. The PB suffix does NOT refer to Prototipo Boxer – the factory didn't even consider the engine was a boxer at this time – as has so often been alluded to in the past – so these letters should only be used for the 1972 version and subsequent cars.

The engine had enjoyed three years of being honed to a tremendous state of competitiveness and reliability, though still it was strange that, even in the years when Ferrari had plenty of funding, if it ran both a comprehensive sports prototype team and a GP team, one or the other would suffer. Maybe this shows that the world's most iconic racing name was never as big as it seemed, but it was common during these years for the GP results to improve dramatically soon after the sports car season had finished. Throughout 1971, Jackie Ickx had had a long, drawn out 'discussion' with Forghieri about the relative lack of ability of that year's GP car, whilst, at the same time, the basis for one of the Prancing Horse's most remarkably successful sports car seasons of all time was being established.

There was nothing wrong with the motor. Enzo Ferrari must have chuckled with glee when the CSI slapped the new capacity limit on prototypes and sports cars alike. It was a situation akin to that of 1960/61, when the English spent much time huffing and puffing about the upcoming new rules in GP racing instead of simply being pragmatic and getting on with it. Maranello had reached the point, at the end of the 1971 season, where the 180-degree unit was developing 480bhp at 13,000rpm in the 312B so, for reliability reasons, it was decided to reduce this figure to 10,800rpm for 1000km races, and even further, to 10,600, for longer events. These two reductions gave 460bhp and 440bhp respectively as maximum power figures.

There was much moaning about the new engine size limit but, to quote DSJ, again from *Motor Sport*: "The decision to run sports car races to a 3-litre limit has been made. Right or wrong it's too late to stop it now; such moves should have been made three years ago."

'Just get on with it' is the implication, and Ferrari was doing just that. The company's financial situation allowed it to snap up the best drivers in the business for a whole new 3-litre 312PB team for 1972. As DSJ also said: "The real losers are those stuck with the 5-litre cars," and this was partly the reason behind a combined approach to Enzo from Luigi Chinetti of NART, Jacques Swaters of Francorchamps in Belgium, Charles Pozzi of Ferrari France, and Colonel Ronnie Hoare of Maranello Concessionaires in the UK, with the intention of suggesting that the 1971 312P be run in 1972 as a factory supported, concessionaire-run, 'B' team. The proposal, even if it got that far, was stamped on by Enzo himself, who pointed out to Colonel Hoare that the costs involved were too great; £1000 for a 312P con-rod alone ruled the scheme out as unsustainable.

A 1972 Ferrari sports car super team was not only likely, but actually bought and paid for. Six cars were to be built, and they would be numbered in sequence following on from the 'new' 0880 1971 car. Numbers 0882 to 0892 (still operating on the old even numbers for competition cars basis) would provide enough chassis to allow the three-car team to work on a cyclic basis running three-on, three-off race by race; a luxury only a well-funded team would ever be able to afford.

To drive these cars, Ferrari gathered together the cream of those available. DSJ again: "It is no surprise seeing Ickx and Regazzoni staying with the team. They know a good thing when they see one and the 312P is a good thing." Brian Redman had been encouraged to join as it was clear that his Gulf Porsche 917 drives with Jo Siffert reflected praise on the Lancastrian as well as the Swiss.

Mario Andretti was down to drive as and when he could, but his place would most likely be taken by Arturo Merzario when he couldn't. Two unexpected drivers were taken on for the third car, the mercurial Swede Ronnie Peterson being the first of these. He was immensely quick but would need to become smoother to remain quick over the distance of an endurance race. The second was Tim Schenken, the Australian driver who had started in the UK in Formula Ford and progressed through the learning formulae until being chosen as a Brabham Formula One pilot; he was considered a canny choice.

Using the lessons learnt from 1971, and incorporating design features required by new rules, the 1972 312PB was effectively a tidied-up, stronger version of the 312P. An increased minimum weight for these cars of 650kg meant that Ferrari was actually able to enjoy the luxury of beefing up the 1971 car's chassis in its weaker areas, which would help with endurance reliability. Such was the little 1971 car's reputation for being a 312B with fibreglass body, the CSI was moved to include in the new rules a requirement that the cockpit area must have room for two seats and be symmetrically shaped. Smaller wheels, of 13 inch diameter as used by the Formula 1 car, were adopted, and this reduced size meant that the bodywork at the tail of the cars could be reduced in height by 60mm. Conversely, the new wheels were of greater width, up to 16 inches wide at the rear, and this led to the necessity for the tail to bulge out at the sides to accommodate the 20mm extra rear track.

The plan to run at least two cars in all the races except the Targa Florio meant that the cars needed to be easily identifiable from the pit wall during the races, so a different coloured stripe was applied to each car – running up the nose, across the top edge of the rear between small vertical fins, and across the top of the bodywork either side of the cockpit opening. Such was the attention to detail of the team that these last mentioned stripes served the double use of indicating to the drivers where they could put their weight when leaping in and out of the cars during pit stops. Pressure on either side would break the bodywork as there was nothing underneath the fibreglass to take the strain. Other details, such as a clear glass indicator on the side of each car to show the level of oil in the dry sump, show that Ferrari was leaving nothing to chance.

The whole team for 1972 was under the management of

the skilled Peter Schetty, who had won the European Mountain Climb Championship for Ferrari in 1969 so convincingly in the 212E Montagna flat-12 car. Chief engineer was Ing. Giacomo Caliri, and under the 'no-expense-spared' philosophy came the best team of mechanics that could be found. The famous Ermanno Cuoghi was enticed direct from John Wyer's 917 team immediately after that folded at the end of the summer in 1971. In Racing Mechanic by Jeremy Walton, ex-Ferrari mechanic Ermanno Cuoghi said that the cars were easy to work on and the testing was done at Fiorano where he alternated on these duties with Antonio Bellentani. "The circuit was less than a kilometre from the workshop but, because we had to cross the SS12 road to get there we could not drive the cars, but had to load them onto a trailer then unload them again at Fiorano and vice versa on return." Of the racing shop where the 312PBs were prepared, he said: "Everything was really clean, a fantastic place to work."

Well before Cuoghi arrived on December 27, 1971 to start work with the team, a 312PB had already been prepared and raced successfully in South Africa at the Kyalami circuit Rand Daily Mail 9 Hours event on November 6th. We have already referred briefly to this race in the previous chapter. In October Tim Schenken had whirled it round the tight little Modena track in a record time for prototypes. It was entered at Kyalami alongside the 1971 car (0880) that had been built up as a new car around components of 0878 that was "worn out," according to Caliri, especially after being crashed yet again at the Österreichring 1000km. Between them these cars dominated proceedings in the final reckonings, but it had been far from clear that they were going to win at one stage.

According to Jonathan Thompson in his book *Boxer*, the new car's chassis number was 0884, although Ian Bamsey in *Ferrari 312 and 512* suggests that it was 0882. *Autosport*'s reporter Jeff Hutchinson described it as a new car "redesigned around Ferrari's latest low profile wheels ... which resulted in around 3 inches less on overall height ... new uprights at the rear indicated minor suspension readjustment ... they were also using Firestone B24 compound tyres for the first time instead of the usual B17 mix." He also went on to mention that both this PB and 0880 312P were fitted with the latest F1 engines. Although there was a pair of outdated Porsche 917s entered by David Piper, Ferrari saw its main opposition as coming from a cluster of latest specification Chevron B19 two-litre cars, one having the new 270bhp Cosworth Vega motor. As expected, the two Ferraris took first and second grid slots with Brian Redman on pole in 0880 0.6 seconds quicker than Ickx/Andretti in the PB, Forghieri having decided that there wasn't any point in Andretti trying to pinch pole off Redman.

Regazzoni made the running right from the start pulling out over a lap lead after 90 minutes. Andretti had a different tale to tell as the PB had cut out within yards of the start, although he had managed to bump start it going again having lost many places. Hard driving got the car back to second but, just after Regga was knocked off by one of the 917s having its own accident resulting in a pit stop for repairs, Andretti found his mount dying and stopped near the Esses. After some work it restarted and lost 45 minutes in all before setting off again. On top of all that Regazzoni was given a 2-lap penalty for having five mechanics working on his car at the same time. It was not going well and a Chevron was leading.

Redman then put the hammer down and pulled 0880 into a lap's lead again by half distance. Ickx was howling the PB along as if it was a Grand Prix and was up to seventh, while, by two-thirds distance 0880 had a 14-lap lead and Andretti had the PB back to fourth. Finally, Regazzoni took the win and Ickx was second having disposed of one of the 917s and a Chevron in the last hour. Hutchinson commented that it all "disproved the pundits who say that 3-litre racing will be unreliable ... Ferrari won using their practice engines!"

Was this all a harbinger of what would happen in 1972, or would there be pressure on the Prancing Horse?

With Porsche out of the World Championship and heading across the Atlantic to the CanAm series, opposition to the Scuderia was to come primarily from two sources: a team at home and from a new UK team. From home Ferrari was up against Alfa Romeo again which was banking on improving its better form seen in 1971 but with completely new cars. Despite the promising results of 1971 with the monocoque T33/3 cars, Carlo Chiti had returned with a tubular-framed car, the T33/TT/3. Many saw this as a retrograde step, and perhaps in retrospect that turned out to be true. From the UK, well-established sports car people Lola, turned out an extremely neat new car, the T280, based on the company's two-litre experience, but utilising a Cosworth DFV V8. This was a brave move, as there wasn't a lot of experience anywhere in the use of these, essentially Grand Prix, engines in long-distance sports cars. Cosworth had developed a 'Series 12' unit for 1000km running and this developed 445bhp. The Lolas were to be run by Jo Bonnier's Ecurie Bonnier outfit, but there was a second marque planning to use Northampton's favourite power unit, and this was Mirage. Born out of the remains of the John Wyer Porsche team and run by John Horsman, the car was by Len Bailey but it was heavy and the company was starting from scratch.

Testing at Vallelunga had shown that the PB was about eight seconds a lap quicker, on a 1 minute 10 seconds lap, than the 1969 V-12 312P, although no-one really knew how relevant this information was at the time. Out again at Daytona, before the season began and in rainy weather, Ian Bamsey says in his book *Ferrari 312 and 512* that a desperate need for some sort of cockpit weatherproofing was flagged up.

Buenos Aires 1000 Kilometers

There was a surprise in store for the team upon arrival at Buenos Aires in the first week of 1972 for the initial round of the World Sportscar Championship. The new Lola was very quick indeed, and Reine Wisell later went on to set the fastest lap of the race. The 312PBs were all broadly as raced by Ickx/Andretti at Kyalami the previous November, with only detail modifications. They ran on 13in front and 15in rear wheels with the latest very low-profile tyres from Firestone. The Belgo-American pairing were in

The start of the Buenos Aires 1000 Kilometers with the eventual winner, the 312PB of Peterson/Schenken (30) and the Stommeln/Hezemans Alfa Romeo (6). (Courtesy Acquati)

0882, Regazzoni and Redman in 0884, and Peterson and Schenken in 0886.

As expected, the team wound up fastest on the grid, with all drivers within a second of each other – on paper a perfect situation – and they were even able to go home half an hour before the end of practice, so confident were

Ronnie Peterson

Peterson was possibly the most universally loved driver, certainly of his period and possibly of the post-war period. He was a very friendly and open person, but his driving was rarely anything but spectacular. His nine Grand Prix seasons included four with Team Lotus as well as March and Tyrrell. He has been successful in karting, F3 and F2. He was struggling to stamp his authority on F1 with March when he joined the Ferrari sports car team in 1972. He then went to Lotus where he started to win, though he never achieved quite the success everyone thought he deserved. He was killed in a start-line crash at the 1978 Italian Grand Prix.

Ronnie Peterson, one of the great drivers of his time. (Courtesy Pete Austin)

Tim Schenken

The Australian shot to prominence in 1968 by winning a vast number of Formula Ford races. He moved onto F3 and, in 1970, took over the place left vacant by Piers Courage in Frank Williams F1 team. He then drove for Brabham, Surtees and Trojan. While having a difficult season at Surtees, he was enjoying his role as a Ferrari sports car driver. He drove Porsches in sports and GT races until retiring to start the Tiga company with Howden Ganley.

Tim Schenken drove a Brabham at the 1971 Brands Hatch Victory Race. (Courtesy Pete Austin)

they that no-one would beat their times. The only intruder at their end of the grid was one of the new Alfa Romeo T33/TT/3s with a committed Rolf Stommelen at the wheel. His efforts annexed the second front-row slot for Milan.

For the first seventy minutes the 312PBs settled down like a train at the front, with Ickx leading Regga and Peterson but during the pit stops Wisell's Lola actually took the lead briefly and Redman was delayed by starter motor trouble. Mike Cotton commented in *Motor Sport* that the Ferrari drivers were saying the "Broadley-designed car was making 50 yards on them through the twisty parts of the track." The Ickx and Andretti car later suffered from more electrical problems as a reminder of Kyalami when the battery isolator switch played up and they ended up in 15th place with it all to do. Meanwhile, it was lucky the cars were so dominant as the handling of all three was suspect, with only Peterson/Schenken not complaining of oversteer, as they'd had their front anti-roll bar adjusted before the start. To no avail, though, as, hoisted by their own petards, they were now complaining of understeer. Added to all this the Ickx/Andretti car suffered a puncture and came in for the rogue wheel to be changed, only to find that the mechanics had changed the wrong one in a display of pit technique the cynics usually expect from an Italian team! Having dragged themselves back up the ladder to fifth despite all the problems, the electrical gremlins struck again as the battery earth lead broke, demoting them to tenth.

Team manager Schetty could at last relax, though, as Peterson/Schenken were able to reel off the final laps in the lead, ahead of Regazzoni and Redman. Schetty engineered things so that the three team cars would cross the line together, and people were left wondering what would happen when the Lolas were better sorted.

Daytona 6 Hours

Maybe Daytona would show what the Lolas were capable of? The 1972 rules governing race length meant that the 24-hour grind would be a pale shadow of itself, cut down as it was to only six hours. As one pundit suggested, this

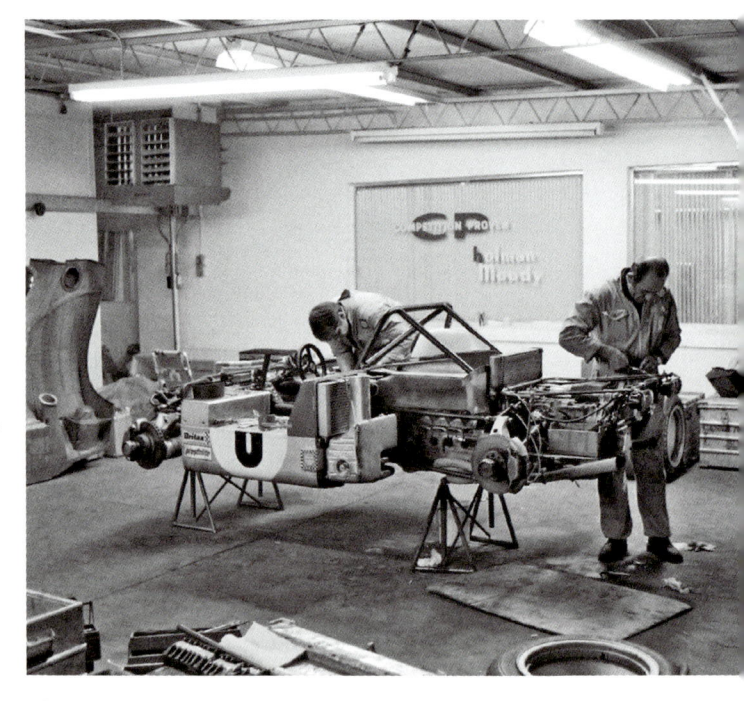

The Ferrari mechanics work on one of the 312PB chassis before the race. (Courtesy Lou Galanos)

was so that the usual meagre crowd wouldn't have to wait so long to see the finish.

In keeping with the one-race-on, one-race-off plan, Maranello turned up with the other half of its 312PB fleet allocated as 0888 to Ickx/Andretti, 0890 to Regazzoni and Redman, and 0892

The Ickx/Andretti, Regazzoni/Redman and Peterson/Schenken 312PBs lead the pack on the first lap. (Courtesy Lou Galanos)

to Peterson/Schenken. This time they annexed all three top grid positions in chassis number order, but 0892 was suffering from clutch/gearbox problems. That was only the start as once again all manner of problems afflicted the 312PBs despite their early race dominance sweeping round in 1-2-3 order.

Wisell and his Lola were once again a nuisance, keeping close and getting amongst them after Schenken pitted 0892 with clutch slip, losing time waiting for the fix. The Lola was quick round the banking and was threatening Regazzoni for the lead when 0890 suffered a puncture, probably after picking up debris from one of the decrepit Corvette backmarkers that were crashing on the circuit and making the lives of the front runners very difficult. Incredibly, during practice, one of these Corvettes, ostensibly in Group 4 GT trim, had been passing the 312PBs on the straight until it was found to be running a less-than-standard 8.4-litre CanAm

The Alfas worked hard to stay in touch with the Ferraris in the early laps. (Courtesy Lou Galanos)

The Peterson/Schenken 312PB closes on the Stommeln Alfa. (Courtesy Acquati)

The Alfa Romeo signals Regazzoni to pass him on the inside. (Courtesy Acquati)

engine! The disintegrating tyre on the 312PB caused the Swiss' bodywork to fly off, seriously wounding the Lola with the result that Andretti went into the lead only to suffer the engine dropping onto 11 cylinders. Mario later commented that he had to drive his car "like a stock-car" just to keep up, such were the low standards of the backmarkers keeping their eyes on their mirrors.

Regga had abandoned hope of going any further with his damaged car until Schetty thought it might be possible to get it going again, so it was dragged to the pits and repaired. Alfa thought this wrong and protested, but the organisers were, according to *Motor Sport*: "So inefficient that they first lost the protest, and then turned it down when someone found it." Apparently, no-one could understand what Ing. Marelli from Alfa was saying ...

There was an element of farce about this race as the sick Ickx/Andretti car led until a routine pit stop put it behind Schenken/Peterson. However, the organisers' timings were awry and Schetty was considering protesting the fact that they had the order the other way around until the latter car suffered a puncture, on top of its gearbox problems, allowing the order to revert to that shown by race-control; and so they finished 1-2. Amazingly, the Regazzoni/Redman repaired car was, by the end, fourth, despite being 15 laps down. NART had also entered 0872, tagged the Chinetti Speciale in its 'new form,' for Chinetti Jr and George Eaton, but it failed to finish.

Sebring 12 Hours

The next race on the schedule was at Sebring but, before this could happen, there was the traditional Le Mans Test Weekend in France. Ferrari took two cars, *Autosport* claiming that one was the original Kyalami PB 0884 and the other, apparently, a brand new car, possibly 0894.

Ferrari's intention to race in the 24 Hours was by no means definite but, just in case, it had made up two new tails, both long and longer, to cope with the high speeds on the Mulsanne Straight. One was a full 980mm extension over standard, with four vertical fins carrying adjustable wings, while an intermediate version was 120mm longer than the usual abbreviated tail. The longer design produced instability at full speed so Ickx wound up fastest with one of the intermediates fitted, clocking 314kph. It was reported that Merzario had a stopwatch fitted to his steering wheel in the second car, with the comment that it must have been quite difficult operating it to check maximum speed while steering down the ligne droite at over 300kph.

The next week everyone was back in the States for Sebring testing with the Buenos Aires cars as per the rotating plan, although front brake-sized disks had been fitted to the rear of all cars to cope with the circuit's demands. That the whole sports car effort was deadly serious was pointed out by Schetty when he told journalists that this exercise was costing Ferrari about $35,000 at contemporary prices. This was more than the total prize money pot on offer to competitors at the very rough Floridian race track.

Because the circuit was in such a 'well-used' state and the race was scheduled for the traditional 12 hours, it was clear that the word endurance was going to describe the event more clearly than just a race. Pete Lyons in his *Road and Track* report stated that: "All four Alfas more or less fell apart," and the Lola "disintegrated time and time again, but the dogged mechanics kept patching it together finishing sixth." Ferrari "was the absolute master of Sebring ... they were remarkably durable," but one was not to finish, nor even to survive.

Practice was another Maranello steamroller demonstration as Andretti went fastest on the Thursday, followed by the Regga/Redman car and Schenken/Peterson. By dint of some extremely hard work and hard driving, Stommelen managed to go faster than the third PB on Friday morning but nothing seemed to faze the Maranello squad and they went off to lunch never bothering to return in the afternoon.

Once the race started on the Saturday it was just a matter of the PBs settling into a routine. They ran in qualifying order whilst all else seemed to be pounded to pieces by the dreadful old track. Even the Ferraris weren't immune, though, as first Andretti lost his lead with yet another recurrence of battery lead trouble, then Ronnie had the engine die and had to leg it to the pits for more fuel. This and a brake locking incident left them behind one of the Alfas, and so he and Tim started to hammer the car back into contention. Tim set fastest lap at one point and there was a little traditional Ferrari pit signalling scene as Schetty tried to slow Ronnie while Tim was behind him waving the Swede to go faster!

A constant problem for the Andretti/Ickx car was that there was a serious oil leak from the point where the pump mated to the block. The only solution was continual topping-up every 27 laps which was the minimum period allowed. This let Regazzoni and Redman into a steady lead for a long time that looked as if it would consolidate itself into victory until signs of flames at the rear of the car led to Clay feeling waves of hot air and smoke as he braked. He abandoned ship but the totally inefficient marshals took over five minutes to arrive and by then the car had burned to a crisp. The only thing salvageable was the chassis plate. Schetty made his feelings known when he boycotted the prizegiving later.

Andretti/Ickx had won, but with fingers firmly crossed in the pits towards the end as the team was balancing out not stopping for a final fuel-stop over the chances that the virtually oil-less motor might not have restarted. The car cruised the last few laps while Ronnie and Tim fell in behind to take second.

Brands Hatch 1000 Kilometres

One advantage of having Fiat on your side in Italy is that things could be made to happen. You want an autostrada closed for race car testing? No problem. Heading out of Turin towards Piacenza, the section between the Santena and Villanova exits is arrow straight and, previously, had been closed to allow maximum speed testing of the Le Mans-tailed Ferrari 512S cars; now it was to be used again for the PBs. In a vain search for total stability with the extra-long tail, Merzario spent a Sunday hammering up and down the motorway, eventually cutting the timing beam at 336kph, but the car was still not settled at those speeds.

High speeds were not to be so much of a problem in the next two rounds of the sports car series as it settled into Europe at the traditional Brands Hatch BOAC-sponsored 1000 Kilometre event.

Now that the Championship was on home ground for all the teams, hopes were expressed that Lola, Alfa Romeo and Mirage would be more able to take the fight to Maranello, but the leading team arrived looking stronger than ever. Three PBs as usual turned up, consisting of Daytona cars for Ickx/Andretti and Regazzoni/Redman, while Peterson/Schenken had a brand new car, chassis 0894, built to fill the gap left by the demise of 0884 at Sebring. Though this car's physical being was gone, its spirit remained in the form of its chassis plate. More new rules from the CSI meant that the rear bodywork was required to continue downwards at the back of the tail of all the cars, enclosing the rear wheels.

Alfa came straight to Brands from Florida with only modified engines to play with, while *Motor Sport*

Mario Andretti gets in a fast lap in first practice in 0888. (Courtesy Peter Collins)

commented on the Lolas that: "Only an optimist would have expected the cars to last the distance. Although barely three months old they look as if they have led an incredibly hard life." Such is the difference a small budget makes.

This time, not even an Alfa managed to get amongst the Prancing Horse's finest as the PBs powered themselves to the first three grid positions. In fact, the biggest surprise was Merzario in a works 2-litre Abarth, who wound up quicker than the Mirage and an Alfa.

"The race pattern was established from the first mad rush to Paddock," said *Autosport*, as the three Ferraris led in line-astern never losing their positions until the first pit stops at 51 laps when Wisell's Lola briefly took over. For the first time in the series so far, the red cars were running faultlessly. After 150 laps the order remained the same and they were all on the same lap the nearest chaser being the Revson/Stommelen Alfa three laps behind.

And so it went on until 35 laps from the end when Regga dashed into the pits with misfiring. A lot of fiddling and out he went again, only to dash in again, problem unsolved. Just to add drama the scrutineers entered into a loud and lively discussion about an oil leak that was being caused by a worn differential bearing. The electrical problem was treated by the fitting of a new coil, and 'adjustment' of the Dinoplex electrics.

Clay Regazzoni in 0890 in practice, flashing downhill through Paddock Bend. (Courtesy Richard Bunyan)

Ronnie Peterson was soon down to quick practice times in 0894. (Courtesy Peter Collins)

This side view of Ickx qualifying chassis 0888 shows how similar the 1971 and 1972 cars were, at least externally. (Courtesy Peter Collins)

Mario Andretti was in pensive mood before the start at Brands Hatch. (Courtesy Pete Austin)

Spectators get a chance for a close look at the cockpit of the Peterson/Schenken car. (Courtesy Peter Collins)

Peterson looks on as his car is lined up in that rather strange old Brands Hatch collecting area in the paddock, on a steep hill. (Courtesy Peter Collins)

Regazzoni screamed out of the pits seventh, but soon caught the Marko/Galli Alfa for sixth. Disqualification of the Migault/Robinson Chevron in fifth meant another place rise leaving the PBs 1-2-5. *Autosport* commented: "On this sort of form, none of their competitors will win one race this year," while Andy Marriott in *Motor Sport* described it all as: "Just another chapter of the successful Ferrari onslaught on the 1972 World Manufacturers' Sportscar Championship."

Regazzoni leads Ickx in the early laps of the Brands race. The cars have considerable ride height. (Courtesy Peter Collins)

Jacky Ickx in 0888 exits the left hand South Bank corner and accelerates onto the back section of the circuit. (Courtesy Peter Collins)

Clay Regazzoni in front of the car that seemed to cause most havoc ... the Dulon-Porsche. (Courtesy Peter Collins)

Here we see the evidence of the Ferrari/Dulon collision. (Courtesy Peter Collins)

Peterson charges on to 2nd place in 0894, and is seen here rushing through Druids Bend. (Courtesy Peter Collins)

Monza 1000 Kilometres

Ing. Caliri had developed some slightly altered intermediate length Le Mans tails for the cars and these benefitted them to the tune of an extra 300rpm down the straights at Monza for the 1000km race soon after Brands, but there were two surprising features of the race. Firstly, it was raining torrentially at the beginning of the day and continued throughout, turning the race into a complete farce, and secondly, for one lap a De Tomaso Pantera led a World Championship Sportscar race. Perhaps that fact alone sums up a day when, after previously setting the usual top three fastest grid positions, unusually with Schenken/Peterson fastest, the appalling weather produced lakes on the circuit from which no-one was immune. Peterson even managed to slide off at Parabolica in the warm-up. For the first time Mario Andretti was unable to take part due to commitments at home, so his place, alongside Brian Redman, was taken by Arturo Merzario.

On lap 33 both Redman and Peterson spun on a sea of water at Ascari, Peterson unable to continue. The former ground back to the pits where the left rear suspension was rebuilt. An insight into how a race engineer thinks was reported by Ian Bamsey in his *Ferrari 312 and 512* book. After the rebuild Peterson was back in the pits after one lap complaining the car was weaving. "Caliri had to think quickly. What could cause weaving on the straight? ... bump steer maybe ... what could cause bump steer? ... excess toe-in? ... what could spoil toe-in? ... a wrongly fitted spacer?" Sure enough, a spacer had to be re-fitted and the car was on its way again to third place beaten by a private Porsche 908/3 that had plodded round with no problems. It had led at one stage and Ickx/Andretti had to drive hard to catch it for the win after suffering a long stop with electrical problems as a result of all the water around. It was, as Denis Jenkinson said: "Even before quarter-distance the whole thing had become a shambles ... "

Still, the result kept Ferrari's run of wins intact.

Spa 1000 Kilometres

The races came thick and fast now, with no more than five weeks separating Brands from the next round at Spa, but such was the Ferrari team's attention to detail that old faithful 312P 0880 had already been shipped out to Sicily to test for the upcoming Targa Florio. The track at Fiorano had recently opened for testing and development, but the rough and twisty mountainous public roads of Little Madonie could never be replicated in Ferrari's backyard. Between Monza and Spa, Caliri had spent a while on the island sorting the 312P with raised suspension, a space for a spare wheel, and all the other details that needed attention.

Many kilometres northwards, the main team settled into the Ardennes for the 1000 Kilometres of Spa-Francorchamps.

Tim Schenken on one of Spa's fastest stretches.
(Courtesy Brian Joscelyne)

Jacky Ickx in the winning car. (Courtesy Brian Joscelyne)

The immensely fast track meant all three cars were fitted with Monza tails and the crews were the same as in Italy, while the use of slicks was causing the cars to deviate over the bumps of the road circuit so 'Indy' style Firestones were substituted.

Despite their usual annexation of the front of the grid, Schenken was finding the short wheelbase sports car a very nervous proposition round the fast sweeps. In the race it was enough for Larrousse in the Lola to actually challenge him for third and take the place, but otherwise it was business as usual for the Prancing Horse, with local boy Ickx averaging over 150mph in the lead with Regazzoni until a tyre burst

and the Swiss lost a lot of time grinding in on the rim for a change and a new tail which had also been damaged. The oil tank had also been damaged and was repaired. Caliri warned Regazzo of the danger of the spilt oil, to which his reply was a curt "... ok, no problem ..." before he powered out of the pits.

Meanwhile, the Redman/Merzario car took a lead it held to the end, but Peterson was caught out by a typical Ardennes shower and had what Caliri described as "a big accident." Apparently, according to DSJ, Schetty openly despaired: "Will we ever have a 1-2-3?"

Targa Florio

More Sunday testing on the autostrada near Turin late in May optimised the shape of the intermediate tail and, by so doing, made both the short and long tails redundant; even for the Targa.

Before this race took place, Ferrari tactically decided to send just one car as Alfa had prepared its strongest team yet. Thus, if Ferrari lost it could say the strength of Alfa made it inevitable, but if it won, it could bask in the limelight of its one car beating the whole team from up the road in Milan.

As this was such a unique event, it was decided that the then-current Lancia rally hotshoe Sandro Munari would be one of the PB drivers, alongside Merzario. Munari had never driven such a car before – this was before the Stratos came along – so he was able to try it on the new Fiorano track one morning. In conversation with Sandro, coincidentally at the Targa course, he told us the story that Enzo himself was present for the test and afterwards asked the rally driver if he would like to join him for lunch in his personal room that he had permanently booked in the restaurant across the road from the Maranello factory. Munari agreed but was more than dismayed when he turned up to find he was going to be Enzo's only guest that day. "I was more worried about this than driving the car!" All was well, though, as the Commendatore turned out to be a charming host, and Sandro recalls that their conversation ranged over an enormous number of topics, not just motorsport.

Sandro Munari

Sandro Munari shared his memories at length with the authors:

"I had done the Targa several times in the Lancia so I knew the circuit very well, and it was important to know the circuit even with a car that could not compare with the 312 for power, speed and size. I was under contract with Lancia at the time, driving mainly rallies. In 1971, the Fiat Group was buying Lancia. Ferrari was already in the Fiat Group, so at Lancia we decided it was necessary to build a new car to follow the Fulvia which was at the end of its development, and couldn't compete with Porsche, Alpine and Ford. The Fulvia just couldn't go any further. But at Lancia we didn't have a good enough engine to go forward so the only possibility was to ask Ferrari for the 2.4-litre Dino engine, the 246. The combination of Fiat, Ferrari and Lancia going in the same direction was important.

"We were working together at the time when the 1972 Targa Florio was being planned. It happened that some drivers didn't want to do the Targa – Ickx, Regazzoni – only Merzario really liked it. Also, I had been a good friend of Ignazio Giunti before he was killed in the 312 in 1971, and we had done a lot of practicing and testing at Mugello which is like the Targa. Giunti was driving an Alfa Romeo at Mugello and I was in the Lancia and I remember after the race he said, 'how could you be going so fast?' and he slapped his head! It was an eight-lap race of 66 kilometres each and he stopped on the first lap and had to watch me. He thought the Lancia was very quick. He spoke to Ferrari when he started to drive for them and said if he were going to do the Targa Florio he would like to do it with me.

"After that I was asked to test and set up the car at Fiorano and we came to Sicily a month before the race for ten days, Merzario and I. Of all circuits, this is a hard one to set up the car for, but we had it going very nicely before the race. It was really fantastic to drive that car. For me it was the biggest pleasure you can get from driving a car at a circuit like the Targa. At first it was only going to be one race. But then Ferrari asked me to test and I raced again with Merzario in the 1000 Kilometres of Zeltweg, and then went to Monza with them. In the same year Ferrari decided to go to Le Mans so we tested at all the different circuits to perfect the car for the high speeds at Le Mans. We even tested it on the motorway near Turin because it has such long straights. But nothing is like driving at the Targa. Every meter at the Targa allows you to modify and improve your approach, so each lap means so much work and concentration.

"The car was so easy to drive, because the engine was so smooth, and you could use so much of the power. In a less powerful car you can spin wheels on the tight corners but the 312 was easy to get the most from. We didn't even use a very low gear ratio. The maximum speed we could reach on the longest straight was 308kph, and that wasn't with the highest gear.

Sandro Munari, still doing historic events. (Courtesy Peter Collins)

We had 324kph on the motorway! We used 1st, 2nd, 3rd and 4th gears so the gearbox was very strong, and it was in good condition at the end. The car was fantastic, and reliable, and we didn't have any problems, just had to change the fuel and tyres. That was over 800 kilometres.

"The difference between Merzario and me was that he had been with Ferrari for several years and he was very familiar with the car; but for the Targa it was new for me, even though I knew the circuit well. There was a big difference between the Fulvia with 150bhp and the 312 with more than 420bhp. Many people remember watching the Targa and said I was faster in the Fulvia than many more powerful cars. What was important when it came time for the Targa, was that the training car was set up the same as the racecar. I think there might have been two training cars, but they were all very similar and that made it easier to drive in the race.

"The Targa Florio was originally the only thing I expected to do with Ferrari, so the other races and testing were a plus. The testing was important because it was done so well. Ferrari himself called me three or four times to come to Fiorano to test. This was like being told that you really know how to do something very well. Because it was Ferrari, it was very gratifying."

Art Merzario on the way to winning the Targa Florio in 1972 with Sandro Munari in 0884.
(Courtesy Sergio Febbraro)

The 1971 car 0878 was renumbered as 0880 and used as the practice car in the Targa Florio.
(Courtesy Sergio Febbraro)

The 1971 312P, chassis 0880, was hammered around the Little Madonie circuit by both drivers practising unofficially amongst the traffic, so that they could get the feel of the cars before timing started. When it did, they transferred to the race car, PB number 0884, and set fastest time. The car had been modified with triple-rate springs, and exhausts that were of greater length, as first seen on the Grand Prix cars earlier at Monaco. This latter work improved the torque curve from 5000rpm right up to 11,800. The car was also fitted with two mirrors on top of each other, as Merzario was shorter than Munari.

Ermanno Cuoghi, in Jeremy Walton's book, recalls that Sandro had had only the Fiorano test to get used to the PB so the Targa was going to be a challenge. The initial practice plan devised was to treat a lap of the Little Madonie circuit as a rally stage. The team split it up into sections and, following with a van and a truck, Munari drove 0880 once over each section or stage and then they stopped to discuss it and adjust the car if necessary. It all worked well as the next day in official practice, the times set were very competitive.

Alfa Romeo had targeted the event and sent a full team, so Ferrari expected the race to be a tough one, but two of the Milanese cars were out early, and, after a spin, the Marko/Galli T33 took up the chase driven by the Austrian. Despite setting fastest laps and briefly taking the lead, he failed to catch the PB by 16.9 seconds, a very close finish for the Sicilian race. Considering he had been brought into the team as a substitute, all of a sudden Merzario was going to the next Championship round at the Nürburgring with the possibility of equalling Mario Andretti's hat-trick of wins in a PB.

Nürburgring 1000 Kilometres

Typically fickle Eiffel weather made for a good race. To start with, the three PBs were far from dominant in practice, with a Chevron B21 as quick as Ickx and the Bell/van Lennep

The Ferraris in the chaotic 'Ring pitlane in practice. (Courtesy Gulf Oil)

The start at Nürburgring with Ronnie Peterson leading Bell in the Mirage and Marko in the Alfa Romeo. (Courtesy Brian Joscelyne)

The Ickx 312PB leads teammate Merzario in foggy conditions. (Courtesy Brian Joscelyne)

Ronnie Peterson on his way to a win in 0886. (Courtesy Brian Joscelyne)

Mirage taking pole. It was initially very wet for the race but the Mirage team gambled on intermediate tyres and took the battle to the Ferraris which were on wets. As the track dried, Bell caught the leaders and enjoyed the sight of Regazzoni sliding off the dry road on worn-out wets at Hohe Acht so handing the lead briefly to Slough.

The Ferrari machine got itself into gear with better rubber and Peterson/Schenken took over the lead, followed by Redman and Merzario. After a variety of problems, from a clutch going solid to alternator problems, Jenkinson commented in *Motor Sport* that: "The Ferrari team seem to spend their whole life fighting off the unknown variables that appear every time they seem to be in full control."

The problem of the Mirage solved itself as, with Merzario hunting it down for second place, its Cosworth engine blew up behind the pits allowing Maranello to take yet another 1-2, although it was still anyone's guess as to when or whether they would ever achieve that elusive 1-2-3.

Österreichring 1000 Kilometres

There was a distinct possibility of achieving the 1-2-3 when the entry turned up at Zeltweg for the Österreichring 1000km in late June. Alfa Romeo had withdrawn to lick its wounds after Le Mans, and the rumoured appearance of the 24 Hours winner Matra remained just that. Many assumed that as Ferrari had all but dominated and won the World Championship it would start to wind down, but Schetty had other ideas and four cars turned up for a mixed selection of drivers, as Regazzoni managed to break his wrist in the paddock so Redman was paired with Ickx in 0888, which had a full Grand Prix specification engine. Peterson/Schenken shared 0894 and Merzario/Munari were back together again in 0884, the car they had used in the Targa. Finally, probably as a test for the 1973 season, a further brand new car, 0896 was made ready for Carlos Pace, who Ferrari had been eyeing up for a while, and local Alfa hotshot Helmut Marko.

Like the Nürburgring, where the grid positions had been affected by rain, the same happened in Austria but

Carlos Pace

The Brazilian confined his early career to successful racing in his home country before venturing to Europe in 1970. He raced an F3 Lotus to win the Forward Trust series. He moved to F2 with Frank Williams in 1971. Frank brought him into F1 with a March in 1972. He then had two difficult seasons at Surtees, but became a very quick if hard driver in the Ferrari sports car team. He had a reputation of tending to drive a long distance race more like a Grand Prix. He became a force in the Martini Brabham but struggled when the team had Alfa Romeo engines. He was perhaps on the brink of improving his record in 1977 when he was killed in a light plane crash.

Carlos Pace was successful in British F3 – here at Brands Hatch in August 1970 – before he moved into F2 and then F1. (Courtesy Peter Collins)

Bell in the Mirage was confidently quicker than the Ferraris and took pole, with only Ickx able to line up a PB on the front row, the middle position being taken by a Lola T280. Neither of these interlopers was able to make it stick, though, as Bell suffered constant misfiring and Larrousse had his throttle cable stick, so that by the time of the first fuel stops Ferrari was running 1-2-3-4. Anything could still happen; and, of course, it did.

Although the two V-8 Cosworth cars were no longer running, Munari was finding the fast sweeps of Zeltweg very different to the roads of Sicily, and was slipping back towards the very fast Stommelen/Hezemans Chevron-BMW 2-litre car. Schenken had the clutch give up on 0894 and Pace took over 0896 only to have vibrations set in. Much to Ferrari's surprise, he was back after a lap and the front wheels were changed – the entire team seemed to be rushing around doing nothing useful, in traditional Ferrari pit stop fashion. Further hiatus ensued when Pace was back next lap with a rear puncture (which was what the first problem had been after all). With the Chevron getting closer and closer, Merzario roared in requiring fuel and a new battery, and left at about 9000rpm, leaving black lines down the pit lane, much to the spectators' delight, and allowing Maranello to finish 37 seconds ahead of Bolton in the end. At last, Schetty was able to record that elusive all-car finish, and, with a four-car team, it must have seemed almost worth the wait. The winning car of Ickx/Redman "never missed a beat," according to *Motor Sport* and "cruised round to a very sound victory."

Watkins Glen Six Hours

Many times during the season Ferrari had spent a lot of effort not just overcoming the opposition but also problems of its own making. Schetty was sometimes beside himself with worry about what of a myriad of tiny trivial reasons could threaten a race win. At Watkins Glen for the last round of 1972 he gave his drivers their head and allowed them to race against each other with no team orders for the first time.

This was all very well but the circuit had been modified and now required both power for the long uphill straight and brakes for the twisty bits, so the Sebring ploy of utilising front callipers on the rear was used. This enabled the cars to go through the race on one set of front brake pads and arguably won them the race, as the Mirages, which were becoming more of a threat each race, succumbed to overheating brakes.

One other modification to the PBs was to raise the rear wing off the rear deck, which gave the cars 200 more rpm up that crucial straight, though at the cost of understeer, which was to become the car's bête noire in 1973.

Bamsey says that Ing. Caliri recalls the race as a cracker, with pressure on all the crews throughout. Andretti was irritated by an engine problem that he complained about when he pitted around lap 30: it would only run properly around 8000rpm. The car was refuelled and Ickx went out immediately, lapping swiftly and well. When the Belgian brought it in for a routine stop, he complained that it would only work at high or low revs, which completely mystified Andretti as this was the opposite to anything he had experienced.

What had actually happened was that the connection between the metering unit and the throttle had broken, so the engine would only run cleanly at medium revs. However, during the pit stop when Andretti came in, he stopped the engine which meant that fuel pressure dropped to zero, allowing the plunger in the metering unit to also drop. So when Ickx restarted the car, its metering and the way the engine ran, was completely different, totally the opposite to what it was before. Andretti couldn't understand what Ickx was talking about until he got back in the car and found out for himself.

Towards the end of the race, most were resigned to just waiting for the finish, though first the Redman/Merzario PB suffered a catastrophic engine blow up, probably due to the crankshaft damper failing. Then Ickx started to catch Peterson in the lead and for the last forty minutes the two drivers enjoyed a tremendous dice to the flag. At one point Schenken complained to Schetty: "Are you going to let them run like this?" as he obviously felt his car deserved the win. "Naturally!" replied the team manager. Ickx won by 14 seconds. "So it was a race after all, although we had nobody but Ferrari to thank for it." said Pete Lyons in *Autosport*.

Imola 500 Kilometres

The race was also on to complete the new PB for 1973 but, despite displaying that the team was well ahead of the game, as in late 1971, the New Year was not to be a happy one for Maranello. There was nothing wrong with the team's commitment as the new car was debuted as early as the week after the Italian Grand Prix at the annual 500km sports car race at Imola. Two cars were entered, for Ickx and Merzario. The former's was the prototype for the following year and incorporated a 120mm longer wheelbase – now 2340mm. This was achieved by lengthening the chassis and, at the same time, 20mm was added to the front track. Bamsey says that Caliri saw the modifications as: "A response to poor balance in fast corners," although the latter admitted that the more obvious approach would have been to utilise a bellhousing spacer. That traditional Ferrari politics were alive and well and still stalking the corridors of power in Maranello is demonstrated by Caliri saying that this latter solution was rejected as too "English." By increasing the length of the car at the front, the weight bias had been moved rearwards.

Perhaps one of the biggest factors likely to affect the progress of Ferrari's 1973 season was that Peter Schetty had announced that he was going to leave the company to return to his family plastics company in Switzerland. It is possible, suggested Caliri to Bamsey, that Enzo thought he was bluffing – those politics again – and when he realised he wasn't, the Commendatore just left Caliri to run the team and be its chief engineer. It was to be a grave mistake. As Caliri said, "... he (Schetty) was one of the best in the business, an ex-driver who understood the technical side ..."

Early rain during practice at Imola left Ickx fastest in the new car with Merzario second. The latter had had little running in which to set a time before the wet weather, so the race, in two heats and a final, might well be interesting.

Whether Ickx wanted to stamp his sports car team-leader authority on the race and Merzario is not clear but, despite taking an immediate lead the Belgian seemed to miss his gear at the end of the first lap and Arturo went into a lead he was not to lose. Ickx then proceeded to turn the heat into an extended test session before taking a fastest lap. This meant he would be back on the seventh row for the final but it didn't seem to worry him.

Although Merzario led at the end of the first lap, the new car was up to fourth as they crossed the line. De Adamich, in a T33/TT/3 Alfa in second, played hard-to-get and it took until lap five for Ickx to pass him and set off after Arturo who had other ideas, too, and maintained his lead cushion whatever Ickx did.

That is, until the Belgian just stopped with a dead engine, opposite the pits. Mechanics rushed across to his aid and it was found the mechanical fuel-pump had broken so he switched to the electric version and set off without even losing second place, leaving Merzario in an unassailable lead for the win.

Kyalami Nine Hours

The season wasn't quite finished yet for Maranello as the team decided to run two 1973 cars in the November Kyalami 9 Hours. 0890, his Imola car, was present for Ickx sharing with Redman, while Regazzoni was back, this time with Merzario, in 0894.

Schetty was making positively his last appearance and this, coupled to the surprise that the cars would be running on Goodyear tyres that were not proving very efficacious, maybe showed the first signs that all would not be that harmonious in the coming year. Goodyears had taken the place of Firestones because the latter company wanted to pull out of sports car racing and wasn't particularly enamoured of Enzo's reasons for keeping it in. The Akron company's rubber was not impressive in South Africa and although the two cars finished first and second, it was not with much help from the tyres, they were as much as 1 to 2 seconds slower a lap in practice than the previous year's cars. The drivers felt that the 1973 modifications had made the PB more driveable, but as to whether it was any quicker seemed a moot point.

With only two-litre Chevrons and Marches as opposition, the PBs should have led both practice and

Regazzoni/Merzario were in 0894 in South Africa, and here can be seen chasing one of the quick Team Gunston Chevrons. (Courtesy Russell Whitworth)

Jacky Ickx at speed in the Kyalami Nine Hours in 0890. (Courtesy Russell Whitworth)

Brian Redman at the wheel of 0890. (Courtesy Russell Whitworth)

the race with no problems and they did, but still suffered from a myriad of trivial problems from which the Prancing Horse cars never seemed to be free. Finally, Ickx' engine dropped a valve, leaving Merzario and Regazzoni to win despite poor handling and brakes, an inoperative clutch, a flat battery, and a late spin on a wet track.

The tyre problem was probed at a Paul Ricard test session before Christmas when Ferrari tried Michelin radials on one of the PBs complete with the necessary suspension and camber adjustments for such tyres. There didn't seem to be a lot of difference between this car and a standard one on Goodyears, and towards the end Caliri tried the Michelin radials on the standard Goodyear car. As Bamsey says "... to the horror of the Michelin men, the times were no different ..."

On top of all his other problems, not least of which was an ever-increasing threat from Matra who had targeted the World Sportscar Championship in 1973 as well as just running at Le Mans, was a big financial problem at Maranello that saw a cutback in the money spent on all competition. Three of the PBs (0882/4/6) were sold off and attendance at races would be reduced to two cars, with three on special occasions. The Goodyear contract ruled Andretti out through his Firestone deal so the two crews were to be Ickx/Redman and Merzario/Pace, with Carlos Reutemann and Tim Schenken helping out when necessary.

Specifications 1972 312PB (where different from 1971)

Engine	80mm x 49.6mm for 2991.8cc 450bhp @ 11,000rpm
Chassis	Wider cockpit opening for two seats. Fuel tank capacity 122 litres in two tanks.
Brakes	Outboard or inboard at rear.
Wheels	13in front and rear, sometimes 15in rear.
Weight	655kg.

Facing up to them was the new Matra team which had decided to develop its MS sports car into one capable of winning at all tracks, not just La Sarthe. Weighing in at 652kg, the new MS670 enjoyed 465bhp from its V-12 at 11,800rpm. It seemed like a competitive package.

Ferrari had taken the 1972 Manufacturers' Championship with 208 points to 85 for Alfa Romeo, and had also won the Challenge Mondiale. Jacky Ickx had been the most successful driver, from Schenken, Peterson, Redman and Andretti. Only Alfa's Helmut Marko had squeezed ahead of Regazzoni and Merzario.

1973 – Ferrari 312PB flat-12 – Ides of March

Sessions in the University of Stuttgart wind tunnel provided Caliri with data for a revised tail section that would provide more downforce. But would the car still have straight-line speed? A call to Fiat and the autostrada was closed again one Sunday, and this time, with the new tail, Merzario clocked 315kph, allied to good stability at last.

Goodyear organised a test at Paul Ricard early in the year and Maranello met Velizy for the first time ending up 0.3 seconds shy of the blue Matra interloper. Not a huge gap, in fact, too close to call perhaps?

Testing at the Roman track of Vallelunga, the location for the first European round of the 1973 World Sportscar Championship, suggested that the new PBs would be competitive, although Ermanno Cuoghi in Walton's book *Racing Mechanic*, suggests that possibly too many modifications had been made to the cars, and anyway, the team was in big tyre trouble with Goodyears.

There were mixed messages from Enzo over the team's participation. At first he said that Ferrari would not be defending its 1972 success, then later in the year the team went to Le Mans so as not to lose out on a possibility of points. Perhaps by that time he was so embarrassed by Ferrari's appalling F1 season that he saw success with the sports cars as a positive way to end the season.

So, no cars were sent to Daytona. This had reverted to a 24-hour event and the one Matra present suffered a spectacular blow-up. As Sebring and Brands Hatch were cancelled, Italy and France first came face-to-face, rather appropriately, near Rome. As it happened, Sebring was taken over at the last minute by IMSA and was run as a Triple Crown round, with a rather scaled down entry.

Vallelunga Six Hours

The pleasant Vallelunga track had never been in the first division of circuits, but late in March the World Sportscar Championship contenders arrived there to do battle. France's 'hotshoe,' Francois Cevert, was inserted into the 'hare' Matra during practice and promptly dealt Ferrari a body blow by going nearly 2 seconds faster – on a 70-second lap. Caliri admits that it did Ferrari morale no good at all as the team had generated a "winning mentality," and when "demoralised, Ferrari starts falling apart ..." as has been seen so often. However, there was some hope in that the rest of the French team was no quicker than Maranello ... interestingly, all the Ferraris and the other Matra, were in the 70-second bracket.

The start of the race at Vallelunga, with Ickx and Merzario in 0888 and 0892. (Courtesy Ed McDonough)

The race showed that the PB was no match for the balance and good handling of the MS670. The Ferraris carried less weight on their front wheels and, with the tight corners of the circuit and not a lot of aerodynamic downloud, their front tyres suffered leading to understeer.

Ickx, in fact, initially led, but soon was overcome with tyre problems. Eventually, the team juggled with springs and rear bodywork with all the cars until Matra had a two lap lead ... then it blew up!

The three Ferraris were crewed by Ickx/Redman, Merzario/Pace and Reutemann/Schenken as Regazzoni was still suffering from his wrist injury. After the blow up, the remaining Matras and Ferraris were on the same lap despite Maranello's problems until yet more tyre difficulties wrong-footed them and a Matra won by about a minute, "... shaking Ferrari out of complacency," as Mike Cotton of *Motoring News* said.

Carlos Reutemann

Reutemann came from Argentina to Europe in 1970, returned home for another season and then came back in 1972 to gain attention in F2. He started the first of five seasons with Brabham before moving to Ferrari for three years. He did a small number of sports car races for Ferrari well before he became one of the team's GP pilots. He's probably remembered most for being seriously inconsistent – he could have brilliant drives on the very edge of adhesion, followed by an event where he hardly seemed to try. He was another thought destined to be World Champion but he never made it. Instead, he went on to become a successful and important Argentine politician.

Carlos Reutemann. (Courtesy Pete Austin)

Dijon 1000 Kilometres

A second new track for the series saw the circus descend on Dijon for the next round, though again this was a circuit not suited to the ill-handling PBs. Apparently, Ferrari management had pleaded with Schetty to come back, such was the company's parlous state, and he had agreed, but on a temporary basis only.

It would take a lot more than the addition or subtraction of personnel to solve the problems, which were basically that the car didn't handle due to pitch changes and lack of front tyre load not helped by running Goodyears. Caliri said that they couldn't tackle the real problem so a deeper front spoiler was tried, only for the cars to exhibit sudden tendencies to switch from understeer to oversteer, and vice versa. After the Matras had secured the front row, Ickx found that the new nose was rubbing badly on the front tyres during the race, so the team had to switch back to standard bodywork.

Whilst Redman was in the car it suffered a rear puncture opposite the pits, and this, coupled with the pit delay, annoyed Ickx to the point where he decided he had to win the race almost single-handedly. His refusal to vacate the car at subsequent pit stops caused Schetty to remark: "He must be crazy!" and made him run back to his road car to check through the FIA book for the length of time a driver was allowed to drive without relief. Nevertheless, the PB was ahead of the second Matra and in second place, although neither Ickx nor Redman were able to dent the time cushion of the leaders, Pescarolo/Larrousse. Considering their delays and the less than perfect car, Ickx and Redman drove well to take second, while Merzario/Pace were forced to nurse their overheating car into fourth.

Monza 1000 Kilometres

Perhaps Monza on Liberation Day in Italy might provide Ferrari with some relief. As strikes at the factory had precluded the team's presence at the Le Mans test days, a new 'coda lunga' was tested at the Milanese circuit.

Monza means wide open spaces and fast corners, with none of the more artificial character of Vallelunga and Dijon, so Maranello hoped to take the fight solidly to Velizy in the 1000 Kilometres. Helped by the fact that none of the Grand Prix-inspired chicanes would be in use, the extra 200mm long tail, sweeping down behind the rear wheel line and with a lower wing incorporating four supports, should prove effective. On the straights these cars could reach 11,800rpm and, because of the longer wheelbase of the 1973 cars, stability was improved over the previous longer tail.

Three PBs were entered and Ickx/Redman were at last able to take the battle to the blue cars, winding up fractions

The start of the Monza 1000 Kilometres with the Ferraris of Ickx/Regazzoni (1), Peterson/Schenken (2) and Redman/Merzario (3) on the left, with two Matras on the right. (Courtesy Publifoto)

slower than Cevert/Beltoise on the front row, with the other two PBs in line behind on the grid.

What few people know is that Caliri had tried a radical approach to shifting weight up front by fitting 40kg lead bars across the front of each Ferrari in the bulkhead area. It worked well enough, but, as Bamsey said: "When Enzo heard about it, he was furious!"

Ickx took an immediate lead but soon succumbed to Beltoise. Unlike previous races, though, the French were not allowed to draw away. The PB seemed to be enjoying better fuel consumption and Ickx regained the lead during the first pit stops, only to lose it again when Beltoise crept past and eked out a four-second lead. Merzario parked-up when he felt vibrations, and Schenken moved into second place. The pace was furious and the race absorbing. The lead seesawed back and forth between PB and MS670 until wheel hub and clutch problems slowed Velizy allowing Maranello, in the shape of Ickx, fired up again, to slow the pace well in the lead. Reutemann in second place had one of his 'moments,' when, with overheating obvious, he continued to drive on flat-out and oblivious until pit signs slowed him. The average race speed had been a staggering 242.47kph, with fastest lap to Matra at 252.

So, despite the fact that the PBs were obviously suffering in comparison to the Matras, Ickx/Redman's consistency meant that Ferrari was actually leading the World Championship for Makes with 65 points against 52.

Spa 1000 Kilometres

That the race doesn't always go to the swift was amply proven at Spa. Ickx was at home and determined. In practice he put in a shatteringly fast lap of 3 minutes 12.7 seconds, a speed of 263.4kph (163.7mph). It stands as the fastest lap of a road circuit ever. Standing at Stavelot, Denis Jenkinson was moved to write: "They are racing drivers at work, as distinct from drivers who drive racing cars for work ... it was soul-stirring stuff to watch and hear."

Pescarolo was just over a second adrift, and the second PB another second and a half behind, but meanwhile, the Mirages were putting up some good times as well.

The Matras and Ferraris at the front of the grid at Spa. (Courtesy Brian Joscelyne)

At first, Pescarolo simply drove away from Ickx, confounding practice form and demoralising the Belgian a little. The latter gained the lead when the Matra suffered tyre failure and the second PB was in third place having had starter motor problems in the pit stop.

It seemed then that the lead Ferrari needed only to stay out to win when, suddenly and with no warning, it stopped; the gearbox had seized. Ermanno Cuoghi explained to Jeremy Walton that: "The oil coolers were cracking. We started losing all the oil through the gearbox oil cooler. It was new for this race, with little testing. The neck was weaker than previously."

The mechanics had to fit a second cooler on the other car to get around the problem, but not before it had lost fourth and fifth gears. In the pits one of the mechanics was knocked unconscious when the car's tail fell on his head!

All of this had created the classic tortoise and hare situation that underlined that other cliché; to finish first, first you must finish. Despite problems of their own, the two Mirages annexed first and second to the surprise of their teams. Although Ickx/Redman had failed to finish for the first time in 1973, Matras had suffered as well, so Ferrari emerged from this disaster still eleven points in the lead of the Championship.

Co-author of this book Ed McDonough was in that Spa race. He was driving a Dulon-FVC (though not the Dulon-Porsche which had caused such headaches for the Ferraris in the past two seasons!). However, he had his Ferrari moment. In practice, and this is on the long, 'old' circuit, the Dulon had a tyre start to deflate on the long swerving return from Stavelot. He remembers one of the PBs coming up behind him, and didn't want to brake hard at high speed. It turned out to be Carlos Pace who first dodged to the right, then was on the left as the Dulon held station in the centre

Brian Redman comes in for his stop at Spa. 0888 failed to finish. (Courtesy Brian Joscelyne)

MARTINI
PRESSE
Shell Shell

ESSO
ESSO
ESSO
Chevron
TEXACO
CHAMPION
Shell
Shell
GOODYEAR
DUNLOP
BILSTEIN

Carlos Pace passes the Spa pits. (Courtesy Brian Joscelyne)

of the road, and then the Ferrari whipped past on the right, on the grass: "I went to apologise to Carlos back in the pit-lane, told him what happened. He smiled and said: 'What?' He hadn't even noticed!"

Targa Florio

Less than two weeks later the classic Targa Florio was due to run. Again, this was for the last time, and both Ferrari and Alfa Romeo, with their latest flat-12s debuted at Spa, turned up in force, this time with rally man Cesare Fiorio standing in as team manager. The PBs were 0894 for Ickx/Redman, and 0892 for Merzario and Targa veteran Vaccarella. Interestingly, Pete Lyons reported in *Autosport* that one of the shorter wheelbase 1972 cars was brought for practice; presumably this would have been 0882 or 0886, unless anyone knows better?

Neither Ickx (amazingly it was his first time there), nor Redman felt happy, but Merzario was straining at the leash and went round in practice only 2 seconds slower than Kinnunen's outright lap record. This was astonishing, as the Finn's mount was a purpose-built Porsche 908/3 weighing 570kg, whilst Arturo's PB weighed 650kg. For the Targa, Ferrari had fitted the required spare wheel in the offside sponson so that all the fuel was carried on the nearside. Lyons says he noted that the engines sported longer exhaust pipes and the suspension was on single-rate springs. Both cars had a radio antenna attached to the rollover bar which, apparently, worked around most of the mountainous circuit.

Regazzoni had an enormous accident in practice, his T33 Alfa somersaulting end-over-end down a mountain. Typically, when asked about it afterwards, he said they didn't think they could get it ready for the race, maybe the next one! Most imagined that might be possible – if the race was in six months time! Andy Marriott in *Motor Sport* pondered on: "... how much longer he could go on getting away with enormous accidents ..."

The PBs never had a chance to show their race mettle as Arturo picked up a puncture on the first lap, missed the intended change point and continued to the pits on the rim. The tyre was changed but the driveshaft was damaged and soon the car was out on the second lap. Ickx was going steadily until, apparently, he rounded a corner in Collesano to find a rock in the road that hadn't been there before. It is vital to stay in the middle of the road on the early laps to avoid this sort of thing but in the heat of the moment Jacky swerved, glanced a wall and was out.

The Alfas suffered, too, with De Adamich being forced off the road by a local Lancia Fulvia, so that, in the end the race was won by a Martini-sponsored Porsche RS Carrera, followed by one of the early Lancia Stratos driven by Sandro Munari and the tough Jean-Claude Andruet.

Nürburgring 1000 Kilometres

The only consolation to the Targa result was that the overall Championship points position hadn't changed and, although Nürburgring was next up closely followed by Le Mans, all the teams realised they would have to be present in the Eifel mountains because no-one could afford to lose any ground in the Championship.

Ferrari had two cars as usual. Ickx/Redman had 0888 and Merzario/Pace were trying 0890. The latter chassis had been subject to some changes at the rear in an effort to ameliorate the balance problem. Mauro Forghieri, who had been office-bound most of the year dealing with serious ongoing Grand Prix car problems, had also had time to have a look at the long-wheelbase PBs. As a potential short-term improvement, he had concentrated on air-flow over the rear wing. The whole tail section was longer and smoother in order not to impede the air as it passed over the wing, and in order to achieve this it had been necessary to move the oil cooler from its traditional position above the clutch housing to a position under the right-hand water radiator, so that the latter still received its air through a duct on top, while the oil cooler drew in air through a new duct set in the side sponson and ejected it into the engine bay. Smooth air-flow was also the reason for the two engine air scoops on the top of the lid, just behind the roll-over bar, being replaced with just one large example feeding into a wide air box on top of the motor. The standard car, 0888, had a balance tube between its two engine air boxes, and both cars featured progressive-rate springs that stiffened to help reduce the pitch problems. The standard car was also equipped with top-of-front wheelarch louvres to relieve wheel rotation pressure buildup; these had first been seen at Dijon. Denis Jenkinson made mention of the fact that 0890 also had new pattern rear suspension hub carriers. He also noted how much variety there was in sports car racing – Ferrari had its flat-12 hanging off a tubular framework, Alfa the same style motor nestling in a tubular bay, and Matra had its V-12 bolted to the car's bulkhead.

As always, the latter's hare, Francois Cevert, went straight out in practice and set a very quick 7 minutes 12.8 seconds. As at Vallelunga, though, nobody else was able to get anywhere this time, and Caliri noted that the Matra team "... have a Formula One mentality ..."

In fact, it proved difficult for anyone to get round within seven seconds of this time and the fastest Ferrari, that of Ickx, was only on 7 minutes 21.7. The organisers had said 15.5 but their times were suspect for the whole of practice. Pace commented that Forghieri's alterations to 0890 didn't seem to have made much difference and this car was slower than its sibling.

A relieved Ferrari team was pleased to hear that Pescarolo's Matra had only got as far as Schwedenkreuz before its engine exploded, but Cevert came past at the end of the first lap with 6.3 seconds in hand over Ickx, and Merzario was only yards behind. The gap extended until Ferrari breathed easy when the leader suffered a rod breakage out in the country at the Wippermann.

With relief, Caliri hung out a 'hold station easy' sign to his two cars to ensure victory, but Merzario had other ideas

Ickx (1) and Merzario (2) at the start of the Nürburgring 1000km, fighting with the Matras of Cevert and Pescarolo, and the new 12-cylinder Alfas of Stommeln and Regazzoni. (Courtesy Ed McDonough)

and broke the rules by catching Ickx and even overtaking him at one point to the apoplexy of the team. To make his point, he very obviously waited until they were passing the main grandstand before waving the Belgian back into the lead. Caliri was so angry that, when Arturo came in to hand back to Pace, he forcibly dragged the little driver from

Como out of the car and told him loudly what he thought there and then!

Ed McDonough was making another appearance in the Dulon-FVC with Dr. Tony Goodwin at the 'Ring. While he had a chance to observe the 312PBs in practice – as they went by very quickly – Goodwin moved over in the early

Co-author Ed McDonough was driving in this race, and caught Pace leaving the pits in 0892. (Courtesy Ed McDonough)

laps of the race to let the flying Cevert past. Goodwin went off the road and wrote off the Dulon.

Le Mans 24 Hours

The 1-2 meant that Ferrari now had 95 points to a private Porsche's 72 and Matra's 64. The championship looked secure, but there were four races to go and the next was La Sarthe's 24-hour endurance test. In addition, the worst three scores would have to be dropped at the end of the series. Would the engines last for a day? They had to run there, they had no choice, but Enzo had always insisted that 24 hours would be an impossibility for these cars.

Anyway, three team PBs arrived at Le Mans. Ickx/Redman retained their 0888 from the 'Ring, Merzario/

Ickx and Redman were unclassified at Le Mans in 0888. (Courtesy Richard Bunyan)

Carlos Pace in the long-tail 312PB at Le Mans, chassis 0896. (Courtesy Richard Bunyan)

The Ickx/Redman car in the pits at Le Mans. (Courtesy Archive Gasnerie)

Pace had 0892, and Schenken/Reutemann the recent 0896. All had coda lunga bodywork, louvres on the front wheelarches, and extra headlights in the middle of the nose. The brakes were outboard and the engines detuned to 450bhp at 10,500rpm. Ferrari's bad news was that Matra had found the cause of the engine blow-ups and rectified the problem, and also had updated MS670B versions as part of its armoury.

The sun goes down on the 312PB at Le Mans. This is Carlos Pace at night. (Courtesy Ferret Fotographic)

The cars managed 332kph on the Mulsanne and Merzario/Pace were fastest of all at 3 minutes 37.5 seconds, just over two seconds faster than the quickest Matra. The Ferrari drivers reported that the Velizy cars were slightly quicker on the straight but worse at braking. Probably because he had little choice, Caliri designated the Merzario/Pace car as hare and a gleeful Merzario as first driver.

Arturo drew out four seconds lead on the first lap (!) and extended this to forty after an hour. Cevert was behind him but, after taking over, Pace was soon back in the pits with a broken fuel collector pot. Cuoghi, quoted in Walton's book, stated: "... we have a small collector pot in the fuel system that was a bit too big for the vibration the car suffered on the straight. We did not do 24-hour tests at Fiorano at that speed so it really was not proved. These pots started splitting and we replace them a lot of times ..."

It was swings and roundabouts, though, as Matra went into a good lead, only to lose it late in the evening after tyre blow-outs. By midnight, Ferraris were first and second with Schenken/Reutemann in the lead and Ickx/Redman a very careful second.

First surprise and disappointment for Maranello came at 02.30 Sunday when Reutemann coasted in with a dead engine. Apparently all had been fine when it had suddenly stopped ... the engine was finished and it was pushed away. Carlos reckoned that the low rev limit allowed for the cars had set up unwanted vibrations.

Vibrations were probably the reason for the leading Ickx/Redman PB slowing and sounding awful about 08.00 Sunday. The exhaust was becoming detached on one side and this was to lead to later valve trouble and ultimate retirement, but not until 14.30 Sunday with the finish in sight and still in a battle for the lead as it was on the same lap as Matra. Merzario/Pace suffered another split collector pot but kept everything together to finish second, nearly six laps down.

In *Motor Sport* Andy Marriott said: "It was a great victory for Matra but one that had not come easily." *Autosport* commented that when the Ickx car retired "... like a brave fighter that had fought well, the packed stands gave the Ferrari team a standing ovation as they wheeled the car down the pit road."

The winning Matra had achieved its result despite having its starter motor rebuilt during the race which was illegal. The excuse was that the 'engine was rebuilt.' Caliri sighed "... Matra is French ..."

The points situation was still standing in Ferrari's favour but it was obvious to all that, with a new Matra now up-and-running, Maranello would be fighting for scraps with the Mirages in future.

Österreichring 1000 Kilometres

The last round of the Makes series in Europe was at Österreichring and the race can best be summed up by Caliri's quote: "The car was a disaster here." The high speed swerves at Zeltweg had none of the characteristics of the sweeps at Spa, and the PBs showed no likelihood of challenging the MS670Bs whatsoever. They did manage to keep ahead of the Mirages at first and Ickx/Redman finished third even though they had to stop early for fuel due to the metering unit playing up, forcing the engine to run on full rich. The Merzario/Pace car "ran like clockwork" except for bodywork bothers that included a stop, after earlier repairs, to allow Art Merzario to see where he was going. Sixth was their reward.

Watkins Glen Six Hours

All of this left Maranello with only a flickering flame of hope in the Championship. The points were now Ferrari 122, Matra 104, but there was still a visit to Watkins Glen to go before the finale in Buenos Aires. Could the Prancing Horse hang on, or even pull something out of the bag? The latter seemed unlikely, but this was motor racing after all.

Neither team could afford to stay away from upstate New York, but betting men knew that the Matras would start as favourites. As *Autosport* said: "Despite Ferrari's apparent large lead in the championship points they still have to drop their two lowest scores from the total at the end."

Three cars arrived, crewed by the usual pairings, and Merzario/Pace had their Forghieri-altered car from the 'Ring (it appeared to have a slight advantage over the standard cars). Ickx/Redman were suffering many small problems, from a new nose section with grilles supposed to relieve air-pressure underneath, which didn't really work, to an engine change for one that was worse than the original (so back in the original went!).

As always, Merzario was game for a good run and set off in the lead building up a small cushion as he weaved through the backmarkers that were causing many problems for those following. Eventually, Ickx in second place had to brake hard to miss someone and Cevert ran into the back of

The start of the Watkins Glen 6 Hours. It's all about Ferrari vs Matra. (Courtesy Bob Graham)

Ickx was very fast in 0896. (Courtesy Bob Graham)

Carlos Pace holds off Pescarolo's Matra as they pass the Ferrari 365GTB. Pescarolo went on to win. (Courtesy Bob Graham)

Reutemann in 0892 passes the Mark Donohue/George Follmer Porsche. (Courtesy Bob Graham)

Brian Redman had a lurid spin but recovered to finish 2nd with Ickx. (Courtesy Bob Graham)

Art Merzario brought 0890 to 3rd with Pace. (Courtesy Bob Graham)

Tim Schenken, with Reutemann, failed to finish. (Courtesy Bob Graham)

him, damaging the Matra's nose and bending Ickx's exhaust pipes. The Belgian suggested that: "Maybe he hadn't seen me [with a grin] but at least I've got strong exhausts ..."

Merzario was finally overwhelmed by Cevert on lap 16, and the Matra took a lead it was never to lose. Redman described his car as a catastrophe waiting to happen ... "It dives all over the road when you brake and understeers everywhere."

Two of the PBs were running on English-made Goodyears, yet Merzario had American-made examples and didn't appear to be suffering much. So often during the season this sort of problem had cropped up, whereby one car would be difficult for no obvious reason, and, conversely, it was sometimes difficult to conclude why another was good. Perhaps there was wisdom in Cuoghi's remark that maybe the cars were changed too much over the 72/73 winter – a classic case of developing a car worse?

That driver/team synergy is important was demonstrated with Schetty in 1972, as many problems could be talked through, though this shouldn't detract from Caliri's difficult job in 1973, of engineering and keeping the team together. Cuoghi: "Caliri has been blamed for 1973 but it was not his fault ..."

Sometimes driver reactions and feelings are so important. Merzario took over from Pace at a pit stop, drove a few laps and then got out, saying the car was undriveable. Pace got in and returned immediately asking for new tyres. It was found that a rear had a slow puncture. Ickx/Redman finished second, well behind the winning Matra, while Merzario/Pace were third. Schenken/Reutemann were forced to retire when the distributor belt broke.

There was now to be a long wait until October for Buenos Aires where Matra needed to finish only third to win the series. However, shortly before the race was due to be held the difficult political situation in Argentina caused its cancellation, handing the World Championship for Makes for 1973 to Matra.

As Bamsey said: "The Ferrari prototype programme fizzled out." Formula One was a more pressing need for Forghieri's and Ferrari's time than another season of sports car racing, and, as it happened, Maranello was on the verge of one of its famous phoenix-like risings from the ashes, as Lauda arrived and the F1 team swept all before it.

Postcript

It's clear that Mauro Forghieri actually continued working on a 312PB update almost to the end of the year for a modified car turned up at Paul Ricard for testing in December. Its wheelbase was reduced to the same as that of the 1972 Grand Prix car, and the nose had taken on a chisel effect. The rear was dominated by a large wing supported on two mountings that ran forward to the air box behind the driver's head in the same way as the 1972 Grand Prix car's 'spine.'

It looked rather like a special based on the CanAm car but, after the French test and one at Fiorano, it disappeared into the factory, never to be seen again.

And finally, NART/Chinetti Speciale turned up at the 1974 Le Mans 24 Hours with another of its 312P V-12-based specials utilising the 1969/70 power unit, but with a chassis designed and built for in America. It was clothed in very neat and attractive bodywork and was driven by stalwarts Jean-Claude Andruet/Teodoro Zeccoli.

Despite managing to break no less than six throttle cables during the race, the car finished ninth and, at one time, around 05.00-06.00 Sunday, it held a very creditable fifth place.

Summing up the Ferrari 312P

Belgian Jacky Ickx was one of the more successful Ferrari drivers during the 312P period. He spoke to the authors at a Ferrari day at the Spa circuit:

Co-author Ed McDonough and former Ferrari team driver Jacky Ickx had a session with Ferrari 312Ps at Spa in 2001. (Courtesy Peter Collins)

"It's a little hard to know what to say about the 312P, it's such a classic sports racing car ... and it has been for 30 years. What I think is fantastic about this particular example is that 30 years after its first outing, it is still in great condition. When these cars are owned by people who like to use them and know how to take care of them, well, it makes a drive like here at Spa a real privilege. It enables me to drive this car in a very relaxed way. Why should I drive it any other way? I don't have to work hard and there is no reason to overly push it. This is a very special piece of history and needs to be preserved. Still it is very fast. It is the kind of car that is naturally quick when you are smooth and if I am relaxed, it seems to go quite quickly, though I am certainly not trying to make it go quickly!

The late Clay Regazzoni recollects difficult moments with Dulons ... Regazzoni on the right, with Martin Ridehalgh, on the left. Ed McDonough, who also drove a Dulon-FVC, is behind Regazzoni. (Courtesy Peter Collins)

"In many respects, the 312 is like a toy ... it is so easy to drive. I have so many good memories of it, having shared it in so many 500- and 1000-kilometre races, and, of course, it had many successes. It didn't win every time, of course, but it was almost always a very good car to drive over long distances, no matter what kind of circuit. In the early days of those cars, in 1971, I remember even at Sebring with Mario Andretti when we were up against the Porsche 917 with 2 more litres, that we were second on the grid; and the car was so good in the fast corners and on the brakes, that at one time we had a five-lap lead on the Porsches and the Ferrari 512M. It was not only a nice classic car but it worked from the very beginning.

"Then at Brands Hatch, which was a totally different kind of track, we were first in qualifying, that was with Clay (Regazzoni) and we were forced off the circuit by a slower car and actually pushed the nose of the Ferrari into the bank. We lost eight laps while the team tried to repair it and, even in the wet, we came back to second place. Even with a jammed starter we were the fastest car and almost caught the Alfa which eventually won. With a car like that you remember how nice it was to drive.

"At Monza and Spa that year we didn't finish, having accidents in these races; but we were always in front in qualifying and usually were leading or were in the front, and the car was only just being developed then. At the Nürburgring it was on pole and well in the lead when Clay had to retire when the engine had a problem. At the Österreichring we were in the lead ... that was when Pedro (Rodriguez) drove so well ... when Clay had an accident, but the car had been in the lead by three laps. I thought we would win the last race of the year at Watkins Glen ... this was with Mario again ... but this time the starter jammed when we were in the lead.

"Then, of course it all got sorted out for 1972 and we won almost every race in the car that is now known as the 312PB, though it was still the 312P to us. The Porsches weren't really there by then and the prototypes were all fast. For us the reliability really came in 1972. That is why I remember the car so well and like it so much. By 1972, there were at least three cars running, all with good drivers, so the competition within the team was more fierce. There was Ronnie Peterson, and Brian Redman, Merzario, Schenken, Mario, as well as Clay and myself – so it was harder.

"The first race that year was a tough one, in Buenos Aires, between Ronnie and Tim, and Clay and Brian. I was with Mario but Mario had to stop on the circuit to fix an electrical problem, so we lost a lot of time. When we got to Daytona, though, the car was perfect and we not only captured the pole but won by two laps. That was a very good race for us. Everything seemed to go on from there for Mario and I. We won again at Sebring by two laps, again we beat Ronnie and Tim. The same thing happened at Brands Hatch with the same first and second, though only by one lap this time! At Monza I was with Clay and the Porsche got between us and Ronnie and Tim and they had some problems too. At Spa we were second because we had a flat tyre, but really we did so well that year.

"Ferrari won the Manufacturers' Championship by a long way and I was the highest scoring driver from Tim Schenken and Ronnie Peterson. The Ferrari drivers were 7 of the top 8 ... that's how good the car was.

"People often ask me these days what I think of the new Ferraris, the modern Formula One cars. I have driven the new cars but it is another world for me. You really have to learn the new systems. The new cars are very comfortable, but you need very different reactions. I find the new F1 Ferrari very comfortable and it has a lot of stability but it took time to get used to the gear change and the way the steering and brakes are assisted.

"I found it nice to drive, and it is not hard to drive fast, but to go very fast, I think that is very difficult. The car is light ... not heavy at all ... but I am absolutely convinced you must learn a new approach. It does feel nice to drive these modern cars but it is not easy. Maybe if I had a chance to do it more often, I would be quicker! But I always loved the cars we drove in those days, the 312P especially."

Specifications
1973 312PB (where different from 1972)

Engine	460bhp @ 11,000rpm. Le Mans: 450bhp @10,500rpm. 0890 had oil radiator on right side and central engine air-scoop.
Wheels	11.0 x 13in front and 17.0 x 13 or 15in rear. Goodyears 9.00/20.00-13 front, 14.00/24.00-13 or 15 rear.
Wheelbase	2380mm
Track	1425mm front; 1448mm rear
Length	3890mm
Width	1960mm

Appendix 1 – List of races

Date	Event	Drivers	Chassis	Result	Race #
1969					
22/3	Sebring	Amon/Andretti	0868	2nd	25
13/4	Brands Hatch	Amon/Rodriguez	0870	4th	60
			0868	DNA	
23/4	Monza	Rodriguez/Schetty	0868	DNF	2
		Andretti/Amon	0870	DNF	1
11/5	Spa	Rodriguez/Piper	0870	2nd	8
		Andretti/Schetty	0868	DNA	9
1/6	Nürburgring	Amon/Rodriguez	0870	DNF	7
14-15/6	Le Mans	Rodriguez/Piper	0870	DNF	18
		Amon/Schetty	0872	DNF	19
		Muller/Williams	DNA	59	
	Le Mans test	Amon	0870	5th	
14/9	Bridgehampton	Rodriguez	0870	5th	12
1970					
31/1-1/2	Daytona	Posey/Parkes	0872	4th	24
		Adamowicz/Piper	0870	5th	23
21/3	Sebring	Parkes/Parsons	0872	6th	22
		Adamowicz/Chinetti Jr	0870	DNF	23
				DNA	26
13-14/6	Le Mans	Parsons/Adamowicz	0872	NC	57
		Posey/Adamowicz	0870	DNS	39
1971					
10/1	Buenos Aires	Giunti/Merzario	0874	DNF	24
31/1-1/2	Daytona	Garcia Vega/Chinetti Jr De Cadenet	0872	5th	21

Date	Event	Drivers	Chassis	Result	Race #
20/3	Sebring	Chinetti Jr/Eaton	0872	8th	21
		Andretti/Ickx	0878	DNF	25
4/4	Brands Hatch	Andretti/Ickx	0878	2nd	51
25/4	Monza	Ickx/Regazzoni	0878	DNF	15
9/5	Spa	Ickx/Regazzoni	0878	NRF	1
20/5	Nürburgring	Ickx/Regazzoni	0878	DNF	15
27/6	Österreichring	Ickx/Regazzoni	0878	NRF	7
24/7	Watkins Glen	Andretti/Ickx	0878	DNF	40
12/9	Imola	Regazzoni	0878	1st heat DNF Final	
6/11	Kyalami	Regazzoni/Redman	0878/0880	1st	6
		Andretti/Ickx	0882	2nd	5

1972

Date	Event	Drivers	Chassis	Result	Race #
9/1	Buenos Aires	Peterson/Schenken	0886	1st	30
		Regazzoni/Redman	0884	2nd	32
		Andretti/Ickx	0882	10th	28
6/2	Daytona	Andretti/Ickx	0888	1st	2
		Peterson/Schenken	0892	2nd	6
		Regazzoni/Redman	0890	4th	4
		Chinetti Jr/Eaton (* Chinetti Speciale)	0872*	DNF	21
19/3	Le Mans 4 Hours	Ickx	0880	DNS1	
		Merzario		DNS	2
25/3	Sebring	Andretti/Ickx	0882	1st	2
		Peterson/Schenken	0886	2nd	3
		Regazzoni/Redman	0884	NRF	4
16/4	Brands Hatch	Andretti/Ickx	0888	1st	11
		Peterson/Schenken	0894	2nd	10
		Regazzoni/Redman	0890	5th	9
25/4	Monza	Ickx/Regazzoni	0882	1st	1
		Peterson/Schenken	0886	3rd	2
		Redman/Merzario	0884	DNF	3
7/5	Spa	Redman/Merzario	0890	1st	3
		Ickx/Regazzoni	0888	2nd	1
		Peterson/Schenken	0894	NRF	2
21/5	Targa Florio	Merzario/Munari	0884	1st	3
		Merzario/Munari	0880/0878	Practice 3T	

Date	Event	Drivers	Chassis	Result	Race #
28/5	Nürburgring	Peterson/Schenken	0886	1st	3
		Merzario/Redman	0890	2nd	2
		Ickx/Regazzoni	0882	DNF	1
10-11/6	Le Mans	Ickx/Regazzoni/Merzario	0880/0878	DNA	2
		Ickx/Regazzoni/Merzario	0892	DNA	
		Posey/Adamowicz		DNA	
	Le Mans test	Ickx	0880/0878	Fastest	1
		Regazzoni	0892	3rd	
25/6	Österreichring	Ickx/Redman	0888	1st	1
		Marko/Pace	0896	2nd	3
		Peterson/Schenken	0894	3rd	2
		Merzario/Munari	0884	4th	4
22/7	Watkins Glen	Andretti/Ickx	0896	1st	85
		Peterson/Schenken	0894	2nd	86
		Redman/Merzario	0892	NRF	87
17/9	Imola	Ickx	0896	2nd	2
		Merzario	0890	1st	1
4/11	Kyalami	Ickx/Redman	0896	DNF	1
		Regazzoni/Merzario	0890	1st	2

1973

Date	Event	Drivers	Chassis	Result	Race #
25/3	Vallelunga	Schenken/Reutemann	0894	2nd	3
		Ickx/Redman	0888	3rd	1
		Merzario/Pace	0892	4th	2
15/4	Dijon	Ickx/Redman	0890	2nd	3
		Merzario/Pace	0892	4th	4
25/4	Monza	Ickx/Redman	0888	1st	1
		Schenken/Reutemann	0894	2nd	3
		Merzario/Pace	0896	DNF	2
6/5	Spa	Merzario/Pace	0890	4th	2
		Ickx/Redman	0892	DNF	1
13/5	Targa Florio	Ickx/Redman	0894	DNF	5
		Merzario/Pace	0892	DNF	3
27/5	Nürburgring	Ickx/Redman	0888	1st	1
		Merzario/Pace	0892	2nd	2
9-10/6	Le Mans	Merzario/Pace	0896	2nd	16
		Ickx/Redman	0888	NRF	15

Date	Event	Drivers	Chassis	Result	Race #
	Le Mans test		0888	DNA	
24/6	Österreichring	Ickx/Redman	0896	3rd	1
		Merzario/Pace	0890	6th	2
21/7	Watkins Glen	Ickx/Redman	0896	2nd	10
		Merzario/Pace	0890	3rd	11
		Schenken/Reutemann	0892	NRF	12

1974

Date	Event	Drivers	Chassis	Result	Race #
15-16/6	Le Mans	Andruet/Zeccoli (* Chinetti Speciale)	0872*	9th	1

Appendix 2 – The cars today

The authors have discovered a great deal of information – and indeed some misinformation – about these cars. This book was intended to provide an overview of the 312P and 312PB rather than a detailed history of every chassis. However, we have included here a list of the chassis and a note about their post-competition history. Our main, though not only source for this information, is www.barchetta.cc.

We have done our best to insure accuracy in the relatively limited space of this volume. We're happy to receive updated information to include in a future edition.

0866 – This was the chassis used for the 612P CanAm car in 1968, and with other engines was raced as a 712P and a 512P. It was with Bob Dusek in 1997.

0868 – Press launch December 14, 1968 in Modena. It was taken to the factory in April 1969 and some sources say it was never re-assembled, and did not race again. Then some remains went to Pininfarina and became a '512S ' show car. It is now with Francois Fabre in Belgium.

0870 – Built as an open car, it had a berlinetta body made for LM 1970 and remained a closed car from then. It went to Pierre Bardinon in 1970 with whom it remains.

0872 – It seems that when 0868 was damaged, 0872 was numbered 0868 for Le Mans. It was, therefore, 0872 at Spa, not 0868. It had a berlinetta body, and was the 'bubble roof' car for Parkes at LM 1970. It was turned into a spyder by Wayne Sparling at the end of 1970. The rear and front end were replaced and the roof removed. It ran at Daytona and Sebring in 1971, then was dismantled, and the chassis and body stored. The engine, gearbox, steering and suspension were used for the Chinetti Special. All original 0872 parts were brought together and the berlinetta restored. It was with Peter Sachs for a while and is now in Switzerland.

The car that ran as 0872 at 1972 Daytona and Le Mans 1974 was the Chinetti Speciale. In 1980/81 C. Conway bought all the 0872 parts, and the non-0872 parts were sold off. The non-0872 chassis and body and other parts were sold on, and had a 330GT engine. It still exists but has no parts from 0872.

0874 – Car destroyed in Buenos Aires in 1971.

0878 – The 1971 flat-12, renumbered 0880, described in detail in this book, is now with Ernie Prisbe in the USA.

0882 – After having an accident in 1972, the chassis of 0884 was said to have been used to repair this car. With Christian Glaesal in 2001.

0884 – At some point the chassis from 0898 was used to repair 0884 when it was rebuilt after its original chassis went to 0872. It has been with Pierre Bardinon since 1972.

0886 – This car was a test car at the 1973 Targa Florio after racing for two years. It then passed through many hands and is now with Irvine Laidlaw.

0888 – This successful car passed to Engelbert and then Christoph Steiger, with whom it remains.

0890 – As with several of the other PBs, this car passed through various hands and has been with Paul Knapfield since 2001.

0892 – This car did several historic events, had a number of well-known owners, and went to Stephen Read in California in 2005.

0894 – This car was owned by Chris Cord in 1976, then Stan Nowak in 1982, and it has belonged to James Jaeger in Ohio since 1984.

0896 – This car was sold to Jon Masterson in 1985, and has been with Giorgio Perfetti in Switzerland since 1993.

0898 – This was an unraced chassis, which was used to rebuild chassis 0894.

Ian Bamsey *Ferrari 312 and 512 Sports Racing Cars* 1986 Haynes Publishing UK
János Wimpffen *Time and Two Seats – Five Decades of Long Distance Racing* 1999 Motorsport Research Group USA
Jeremy Walton *Racing Mechanic* 1980 Osprey Publishing UK
Jonathan Thompson *Boxer – The Ferrari Flat-12 Racing and GT Cars* 1981 Osprey Publishing UK
Steve Small *Grand Prix Who's Who* 1994 Guinness Publishing UK

Journals
Autosport
Motor Sport
Road & Track
Vintage Racecar

Bibliography
Books
Hans Tanner and Doug Nye *Ferrari* 1989 Haynes Publishing UK

Visit Veloce on the web – www.veloce.co.uk
Details of all books in print • Special offers • New book news • Gift vouchers • Web forum • And much more ...

GRAND PRIX
FERRARI

THE YEARS OF ENZO FERRARI'S POWER, 1948-1980

ANTHONY PRITCHARD

An enthralling, comprehensive, and highly readable account of the racing history of motor sport's most important marque, supported by 300 colour and black and white photographs.

ISBN: 978-1-845846-23-7

Hardback • 25x25cm • £85* UK/$135* USA • 416 pages • 214 colour and b&w pictures

For more info on Veloce titles, visit our website at www.veloce.co.uk • email: info@veloce.co.uk • Tel: +44(0)1305 260068 • *prices subject to change, p&p extra

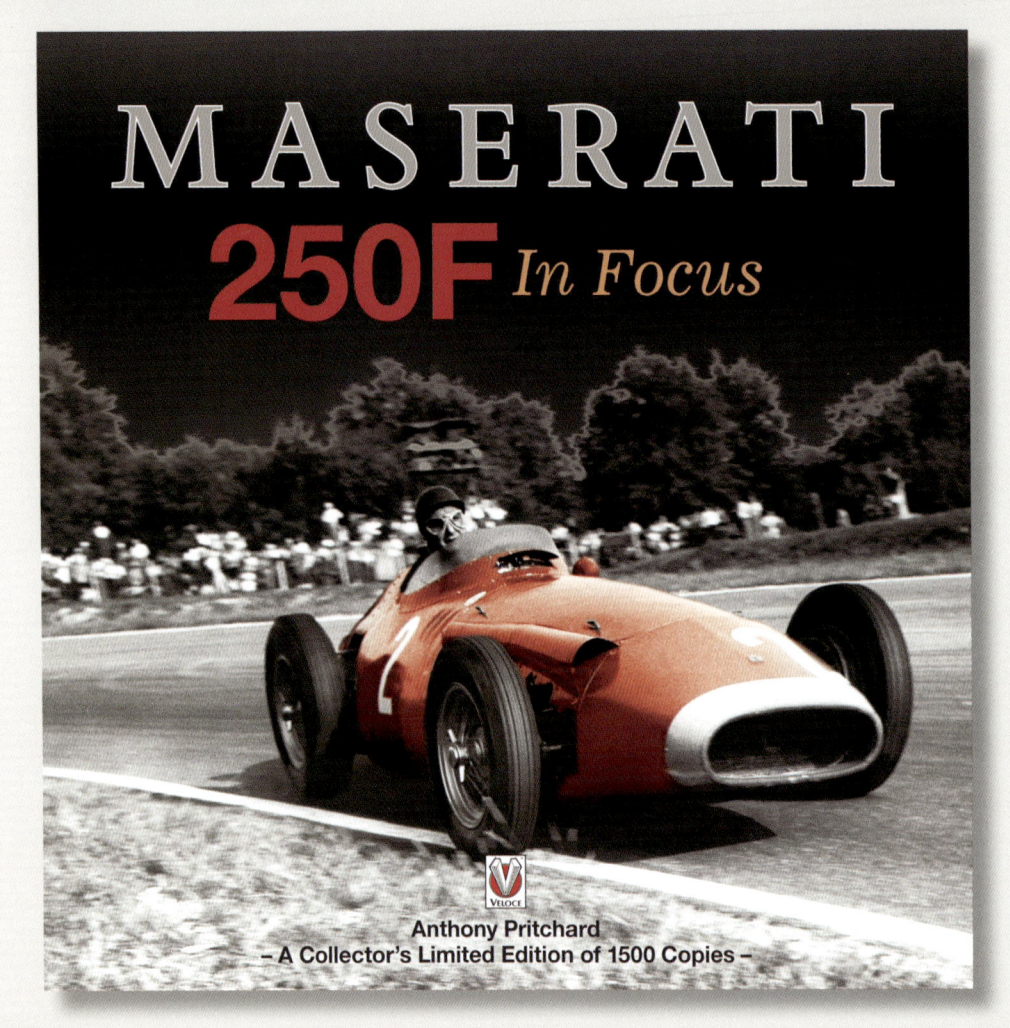

MASERATI
250F *In Focus*

Anthony Pritchard
– A Collector's Limited Edition of 1500 Copies –

The Maserati 250F raced against Ferrari, Mercedes-Benz and Vanwall for Grand Prix supremacy during the 2500cc Grand Prix Formula years of '54-'60. Stories from leading drivers, including Sir Stirling Moss, Juan Fangio, and Mike Hawthorn, bring the racing story of this iconic model back to life.

ISBN: 978-1-845845-63-6
Hardback • 25x25cm • £60* UK/$95* USA • 224 pages • 192 colour and b&w pictures

For more info on Veloce titles, visit our website at www.veloce.co.uk • email: info@veloce.co.uk
• Tel: +44(0)1305 260068 • * prices subject to change, p&p extra

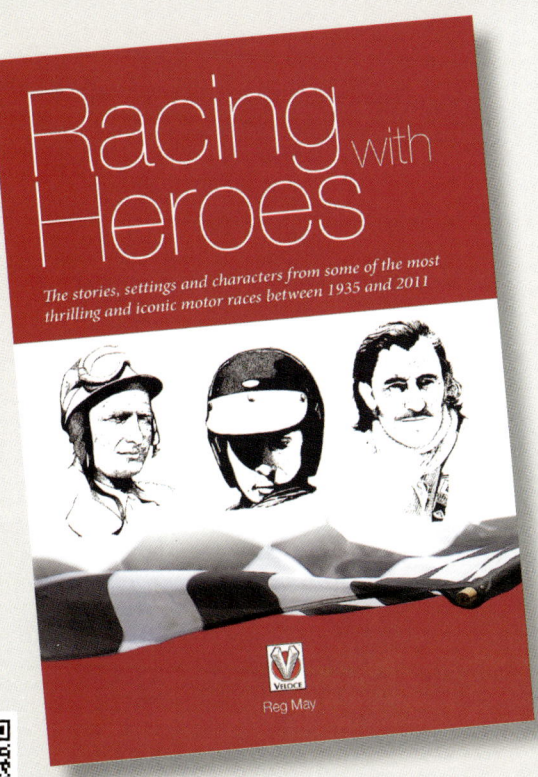

Retells the stories, revisits the settings and reveals the characters involved in what have been the most thrilling and iconic motor races between 1935 and 2011. Featuring such greats as Tazio Nuvolari, Stirling Moss, Juan Fangio, and James Hunt, to name just a few, the book also includes fan photos and memorabilia collected during the era, and personal experiences of many of these great events.

ISBN: 978-1-845846-54-1
Paperback • 21x14.8cm • £12.99* UK/$19.95* USA
• 128 pages • 41 pictures

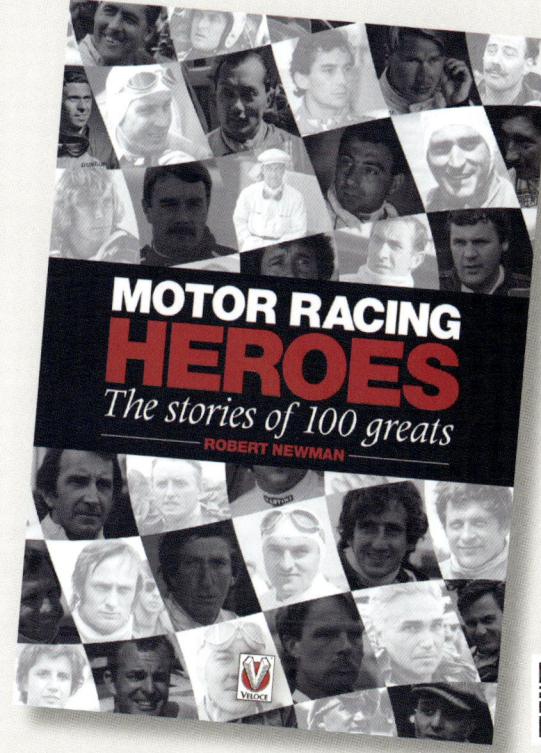

100 heroes from almost 100 years of motor sport are covered in this book. Revealing the determination, heroism, raw courage, skill at the wheel – and just plain humanity – that has elevated men and women into the special, rarified atmosphere of heroism.

ISBN: 978-1-845847-48-7
Hardback • 21x14.8cm • £19.99* UK/$32.99* USA • 384 pages

For more info on Veloce titles, visit our website at www.veloce.co.uk • email: info@veloce.co.uk
• Tel: +44(0)1305 260068 • * prices subject to change, p&p extra

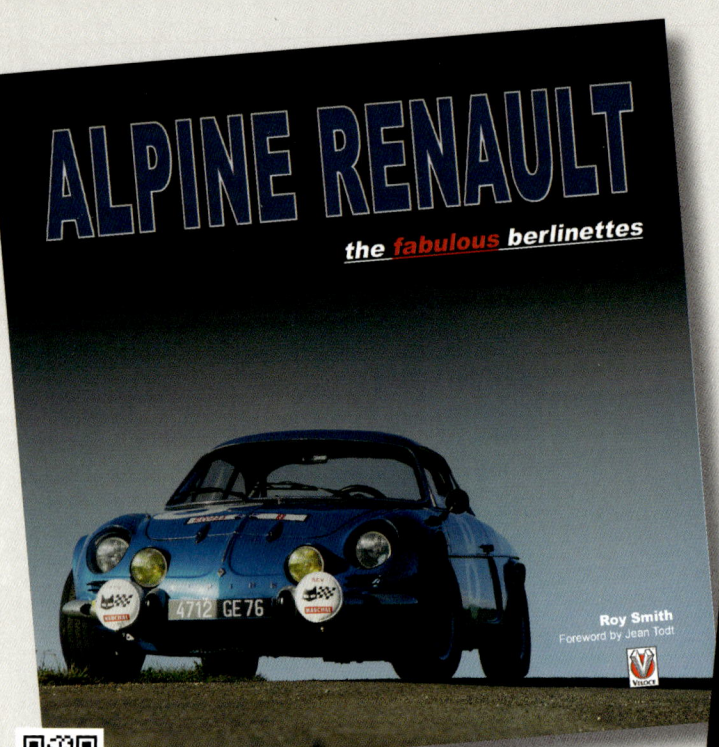

The beautiful design of the Alpine Renault 'berlinettes' and their extraordinary performances in competition made them the cars to beat in the late 1960s and early 1970s. This book brings to life their development and history in fascinating detail.

ISBN: 978-1-845844-04-2
Hardback • 25x25cm • £75.00* UK/$125* USA
• 240 pages • 380 colour and b&w pictures

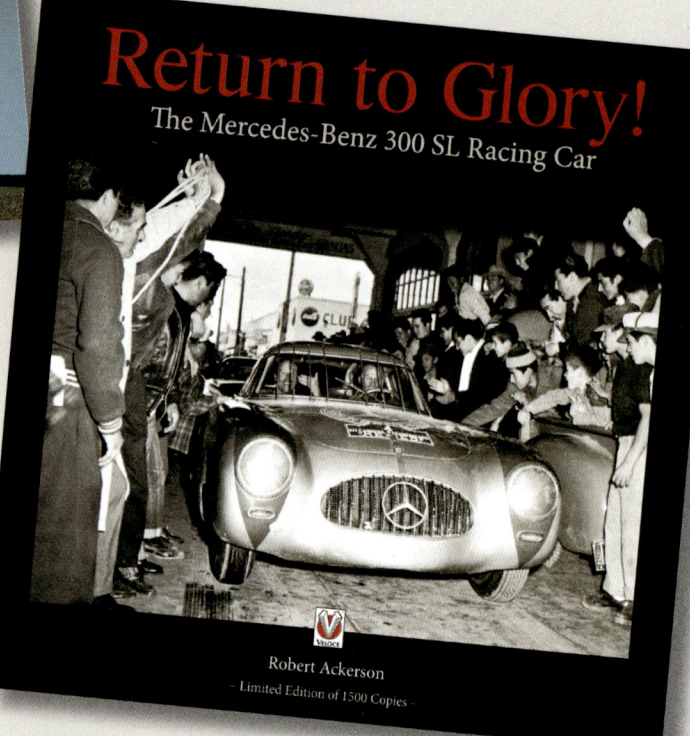

This book vividly depicts the 300 SL's performance in the five races in which it competed in its debut year, 1952. Through dramatic photographs and stirring text, one of the greatest years of sports car racing is brought to life, filled with automobiles prepared by great factory teams, driven by men who were national sporting idols, and raced under gruelling conditions unique to the age.

ISBN: 978-1-845846-17-6
Hardback • 25x25cm • £75* UK/$120* USA
• 144 pages • 126 colour and b&w pictures

For more info on Veloce titles, visit our website at www.veloce.co.uk • email: info@veloce.co.uk
• Tel: +44(0)1305 260068 • * prices subject to change, p&p extra

Index

ACO 5
Adamowicz, Tony 24, 26, 29, 32, 34, 40, 60, 61
Ahrens, Kurt 16, 20, 24
Amon, Chris 8, 11, 13, 16, 18, 20, 21
Andretti, Mario 8, 16, 24, 29, 29, 32, 42, 43, 56, 59-61, 65, 68, 70-74, 76-78, 85, 89, 92, 96, 116
Andruet, Jean-Claude 103, 114, 115
Attwood, Richard 13, 20, 21, 32, 54-56, 60
Autodelta 45

Bailey, Len 72
Ballentani, Antonio 71
Ballot-Lena, Claude 53
Bardinon, Pierre 36, 121
Bell, Derek 38, 40, 45, 50, 53, 54, 56, 62, 89, 91
Beltoise, Jean-Pierre 38, 100
Bianchi, Lucien 20
Binnie, Bill 61, 62
Birchenough, Tony 53
Bonnier, Jo 13, 59, 72
Brabham, Jack 35
Brands Hatch 11, 32, 40, 45, 48, 52, 54, 78, 85, 97, 115, 116
Bridgehampton circuit 21
Broadley, Eric 73
Bucknam, Ronnie 32, 40
Buenos Aires circuit 38, 39, 72, 77, 109, 114, 121

Caliri, Ing. Giacomo 56, 71, 85, 86, 92, 93, 96, 97, 99, 100, 103, 104, 108, 109, 113
Casoni, Mario 60, 61
Cevert, Francois 29, 100, 103, 104, 108, 113
Charlton, Dave 60
Chasseuil, Guy 53
Chinetti, Luigi 7, 20, 21, 24, 32, 34, 70
Chinetti, Luigi 'Coco' Jr 29, 40, 42, 77
Chiti, Carlo 8, 72
Code, Scott 61
Colibri, Ing. 8
Collins, Peter 40
Conway, C 121
Cord, Chris 122
Craft, Chris 60
CSI 7, 69-70
Cuoghi, Ermanno 71, 88, 97, 100, 109, 113

Daytona circuit 8, 24, 32, 34, 39, 42, 54, 72, 74, 97, 116, 121
De Adamich, Andrea 38, 44, 45, 50, 53, 54, 59, 61, 93, 103
Dean, Tony 22
De Cadenet, Alain 40
Dechent, Hans Dieter 42, 54
Dijon circuit 99, 103
Donahue, Mark 8, 39, 40, 42-45, 56, 59, 63, 65
Driver, Paddy 61
Dusek, Bob 121

Eaton, George 42, 77
Ecclestone, Bernie 61
Elford, Vic 13, 16, 18, 20, 21, 24, 29, 38, 40, 42, 44, 45, 52-54, 59, 65, 67
Engelbert (car owner) 122

Fabre, Francois 121
Facetti, Carlo 59
Fangio, Juan 18,

Ferrari, Enzo 7, 37, 59, 61, 69, 70, 86, 93, 97, 105
FIA 5, 7, 24
Fiorio, Cesare 102
Fittipaldi, Emerson 38
Forghieri, Mauro 37, 38, 67, 69, 71, 103, 114

Galli, Nanni 8, 38, 42, 44, 54, 59, 82, 89
Ganley, Howden 61
Garcia Vega, Nestor 40
Gardner, Frank 18
Gethin, Peter 59
Ginther, Richie 61
Giunti, Ignazio 8, 32, 38, 41
Glaesal, Christian 121
Goodwin, Tony 53, 104, 105
Gregory, Masten 18, 32, 40, 43
Gunston team 61
Gurney, Dan 29

Hahne, Hubert 18
Hailwood, Mike 13, 60, 61
Hansgen, Walt 35
Hawkins, Paul 16
Hayashi, Yoshijuki 61
Herrman, Hans 16, 21, 32
Herzog, Rene 45, 50, 55
Hezemans, Toine 29, 32, 45, 50, 54, 92
Hine, John 61
Hoare, Clo. Ronnie 70
Hobbs, David 39, 40, 42, 56, 63
Hulme, Denis 21, 22

Ickx, Jacky 8, 10, 16, 18, 20, 21, 24, 29, 42, 43, 45, 48, 50, 52-56, 60-62, 65, 68, 69-74, 76-78, 85-86, 92-93, 96, 98-100, 102-105, 109, 113, 114

127

Imola circuit 59, 93

Jaeger, James 122
Jenkinson, Denis 69, 70, 85, 100, 103
Joest, Reinhold 20
Joscelyne, Brian 53
Juncadell, Jose 55

Kauhsen, Willy 16, 21
Kelleners, Helmut 20
Kinnunen, Leo 24, 29, 32, 59, 102
Knapfield, Paul 122
Kyalami circuit 60, 68, 71-73, 93

Laidlaw, Irvine 121
Lanzante, Paul 61
Larrousse, Gerard 21, 38, 42, 44, 53-56, 99
Lauda, Niki 114
Le Mans 24 Hours 5, 7, 10, 11, 20, 21, 32, 35, 54, 55, 61, 68, 77, 91, 99, 103, 105, 121
Linge, Herbert 20
Love, John 61

Maglioli, Umberto 8
Marelli, Ing. 76
Marko, Helmut 53-56, 61, 82, 89, 91, 96
Martland, Digby 20
Masterson, Jon 122
McDonough, Ed 40, 43-45, 56, 62, 63, 100, 104
McGovern, Bill 48
McLaren, Bruce 21, 22
McQueen, Steve 24, 29, 35
Merzario, Arturo 24, 29, 32, 38, 52, 59, 61, 70, 77, 79, 85, 86, 88, 89, 91-93, 96-100, 102-105, 108, 109, 113, 116
Migeault, Francois 32, 82
Miles, John 48
Mitter, Gehart 8, 13, 16, 18
Modena circuit 71
Monza circuit 32, 52-53, 85, 99, 116
Muller, Herbert 20, 45, 50, 54-56
Munari, Sandro 61, 86, 89, 91, 92, 103

NART 20, 21, 24, 29, 34, 39, 40, 42, 45, 45, 77, 114

Nowak, Stan 122
Nurburgring circuit 18, 20, 32, 54, 68, 89, 103, 116

Obrist, Albert 61
Oliver, Jackie 10, 16, 21, 38, 40, 42, 44, 45, 53, 55
Osterreichring circuit 20, 55, 91, 109, 116

Pace, Carlos 91, 92, 96, 98-100, 102-104, 107-109, 113
Parkes, Mike 24, 26, 29, 32-34, 38, 39, 121
Parsons, Chuck 29, 32, 33, 40
Paul Ricart circuit 96, 97, 114
Penske, Roger 39, 40, 42-44, 56, 65
Perfetti, Giorgio 122
Pescarolo, Henri 24, 29, 38, 44, 45, 50, 53, 54, 99, 100
Peterson, Ronnie 59, 70, 72, 74-78, 85, 86, 91, 92, 116
Pilette, Teddy 18
Pininfarina 21, 121
Piper, David 16, 18, 20, 21, 24, 32, 34, 60, 71
Posey, Sam 24, 26, 32, 34, 40
Pozzi, Charles 70
Prisbe, Ernie 121
Prunet, Antoine 38

Quester, Dieter 18

Redman, Brian 20, 21, 24, 29, 45, 59-61, 67, 70-74, 77, 78, 85, 86, 91, 92, 96, 98-100, 102, 103, 105, 109, 113, 116
Read, Stephen 122
Regazzoni, Clay 45, 50, 52, 52-56, 59-61, 68, 70-78, 82, 86, 91, 93, 96, 98, 102, 115, 116
Reisch, Klaus 59
Reutemann, Carlos 96, 98, 100, 107, 109, 113
Revson, Peter 29, 32, 40, 42, 43, 79
Ridehalgh 48, 54
Riverside circuit 22
Robinson, Brian 82
Rockingham circuit 61

Rodriguez, Pedro 8, 11, 13, 16, 18, 20-22, 24, 29, 32, 38, 40, 42-45, 48, 50, 52-56, 61, 65, 116

Sachs, Peter 121
Schenken, Tim 70-73, 75-78, 86, 91, 92, 96, 98, 100, 107, 109, 113, 116
Schetty, Peter 16, 20, 24, 29, 59, 71, 74, 76, 77, 86, 91-93, 99, 113
Schutz, Udo 8, 13, 16
Sebring circuit 5, 8, 10, 29, 33, 40, 41, 45, 56, 63, 67, 77, 97, 115, 116, 121
Servoz-Gavin, Johnny 20, 29
Siffert, Jo 8, 11, 13, 16, 18, 20-22, 24, 29, 32, 38, 40, 43, 45, 48, 50, 52-54, 56, 61, 70
Southgate, Tony 67
Spa circuit 16, 32, 53, 61, 85, 100, 116, 121
Sparling, Wayne 36, 121
Steiger, Christoph 122
Stommeln, Rolf 20, 42, 44, 45, 50, 54, 73, 79, 91
Surtees, John 8, 21, 22
Swaters, Jacques 70

Targa Florio 16, 32, 54, 61, 62, 70, 85, 88, 91, 92, 102, 121
Taylor, Ian 54

Vaccarella, Nino 32, 44, 54, 102
Vallelunga circuit 8, 72, 97, 99, 103
Van Lennep, Gijis 53-54, 56, 89
VDS Team 18, 20
Vernon, Michael 61
Von Wendt, Karl 16,

Watkins Glen circuit 20, 56, 92, 109, 116,
Williams, Jonathan 20, 21
Wimpffen, Janos 38
Wisell, Reine 72, 73, 75, 79
Woolfe, John 20
Wyer, John 11, 44, 72

Young, Gregg 40, 43

Zeccoli, Teodoro 59, 114